Creativity and the Jewish Soul
An Exploration of Creativity in the Book of Shemot

by Rabbi Richard Borah

Original Paintings and Annotations by Richard McBee

In memory of my parents Harry and Judith Borah zt'l

Thanks and Appreciation:

To my wife Andrea, for her patience and assistance.

To my Rebbeim, who have given me the Torah- life's most precious gift.

See, I have called by name Bezalel the son of Uri, the son of Hur, of the tribe of Judah, and I have imbued him with the spirit of God, with wisdom, with insight, with knowledge, and with talent for all manner of craftsmanship (Shemot 31: 2-3)

Copyright © 2017 Richard Borah
Published by Observant Artist Community Circle
All rights reserved
ISBN-10: 0692963847
ISBN-13: 978-0692963845

CREATIVITY AND THE JEWISH SOUL

Introductory Essay: Creativity Bound by Rabbi Richard Borah
p.3

Contemporary Jewish Art: the Challenge by Richard McBee
p.7

Shemot: Creativity and Suffering: Confrontation with Non-Being
p.12

Vaera: Creativity, Miracles and the Senses in Religious Experience
p. 29

Bo: Creativity & Compensation
p. 44

Beshallach: Creativity, Catharsis and the Song by the Sea
p. 64

Yisro: Creativity & Boundaries: Allure and Danger of Approaching the True Being
p. 79

Mishpatim: Creativity & Sensitivity: Widows, Orphans and the Justice of Mercy
p. 91

Terumah: Creativity and the Sanctuary
p. 103

Tetzaveh: Creativity, Priestly Robes and Human Images
p. 119

Ki Tissa: Creativity, the Golden Calf and Natural Law
p. 135

Vayakhel: Creativity, Sabbath and the Mishkan
p. 160

Pekudei: Creativity and the Power of Gold
p. 174

Index of Images
p. 187

INTRODUCTORY ESSAY

Creativity Bound by Rabbi Richard Borah

The Torah is our richest source of knowledge about the human soul. Though we each experience our soul's presence every moment of our brief existence, we are primarily unaware of its fundamental nature and operation. This text, and its companion volume on Genesis both focus on the central role of creativity in shaping the soul's goals and pursuits, both for good and evil.

Man is a creative being at his core. He applies this creative impulse to all areas of endeavor. Human history is, to a great extent, the history of this creativity applied to a spectacularly broad spectrum of activities. We highly value those individuals whose creative thoughts and actions bring something new in the world. Whether it is a scientist like Einstein, an artist like Picasso, a scholar like Maimonides, or even a technological "wizard" like Steve Jobs, we stand in awe of those who are able to create something new that expands the boundaries of human knowledge and capability. Rabbi Joseph B. Soloveitchik, perhaps the 20th century's greatest Torah scholar, stated in his essay "Halakhic Man":

> God gave the Book of Creation-that repository of the mysteries of creation-to man, not simply for the sake of theoretical study but in order that man might continue the act of creation… Man's task is "fashion, engrave, attach and create," and transform the emptiness in being into a perfect and holy existence, bearing the imprint of the divine name." (Halakhic Man, p. 101)

But man's creative drive, though central and condoned by God, can also become demonic when it oversteps the limits that the Creator has established for him. What is this boundary that has been set by God to limit man's creativity?

In essence, man is not equipped or permitted to utilize his creative talents to formulate his own set of values; his own morality.

Stepping over this line was the first sin of Adam and Eve. When the serpent tempted Eve to eat it from the Tree of Knowledge of Good and Evil, it was with the promise that she would become a god herself and "the creator of worlds" (Rashi on Bereisheit 3:5) I don't believe that Eve imagined herself becoming the creator of physical worlds. Instead, she and Adam would create their own world of values, and decide through their own creativity and logic, what would be good and what would be evil. In this way they would become "creators of worlds". An example of this "value creation" was the decision that being naked was wrong. This was humanity first independent value judgment, as God did not communicate to them that being naked was at all immoral or wrong in any way.

Although man's applying his creative talents to moral issues may, at first reflection, seem to be a reasonable use of his most central of human powers, the Torah clarifies that the identification of good and evil, and of establishing moral value, lies solely with God. He did not bestow this ability upon man or give him permission to carry it out. Man's role, as defined by the Torah and Jewish law, is to use his creativity to *understand* God's revealed moral system in depth, and to implement it in society in order to "repair the world" of its injustice and suffering (*tikkun olam*) and bring human civilization to full development.

All human creativity and the activities that result from it are to be channeled to this objective. Man's creative focus on technology and science is fully condoned, with these advancements being used to bring to fruition the values of justice, kindness and compassion, prescribed in God's revealed system. But when human beings attempt to formulate their own independent value system, the result is to derail the sanctioned *tikkun olam* process and replace it with a delusional project of human overestimation that will not achieve the form of life that is most consonant with the needs of the individual and the society.

In the book of Shemot (Exodus) the patriarchal family is transformed through the enslavement and redemption from Egypt into a nation whose is charged with the carrying out of this *tikkun olam* process, functioning as a "light to the nations" and a "kingdom of priests". It is for this process that the Jewish people were brought into existence and it is our belief that this transformation will reach full fruition in the time of the Messiah.

Artists brings to the world unique and varied perspectives and methods to express their creative ideas and feelings visually or through other mediums. The scholar brings this creativity to his or her analysis of different phenomena and in developing methods to communicate them to others by words, mathematical formula and technological innovation. But for these most valued of human involvements to avoid becoming destructive to the world and a violation of God's will, the restriction placed on man to not become the independent "creator of moral worlds" must be adhered to.

The Torah is quite clear that all creative endeavors are means to a greater end. There is no sanctioned art for art's sake or scientific progress for the sake of simply making a more comfortable and pleasant lifestyle. Even Torah scholarship itself is a tool for the bringing about of the world's true form as a place of justice, mercy and knowledge of God. Some may chafe at the idea that our creative drives should be governed and routed in this way. But human creativity is deeply intertwined with our ability to choose, and the choice of how we channel our creativity is a fundamental one in our deciding to serve God with this power or to be so intoxicated with it that we embrace the illusion of creativity as a good in itself which cannot accept any governance.

In the following analyses on each *parsha* of Shemot I have tried to address fundamental issues of how the struggle with creativity is shown to be at the heart of the history and mission of the Jewish people. There are poems and painting that relate to the creativity-center themes discussed. Richard McBee, a contemporary artist and writer, has selected paintings of his own and those of other artists which are relevant to the *parsha* analyses. He has also provided annotations on the art selected.

Robert Frost reflected that poetry without rhyme was like playing tennis without a net. I do not see bounded creativity as diminished creativity. As the children of a Creator who bestowed the creative fire within our souls, we are fortunate to have the guidance of the revealed Torah to help us develop and refine this powerful impulse into one that will bring our personal lives and those of the community to a more complete fruition and participate in the fundamental human quest to "repair the world".

INTRODUCTORY ESSAY

Contemporary Jewish Art: The Challenge
by Richard McBee

The Problem

The idea of "Jewish Art" is such a strange and troubled notion. Long denied even as a possibility because of the simplistic reading of the Second Commandment expressing the Torah's abhorrence of idolatry, since the eighteenth century, "Jewish aniconism finally emerged as an unmistakably modern idea." Kalman Bland's deconstruction of Jewish aniconism sees this notion as initially a non-Jewish invention with anti-Semitic undertones—so much so that, "If not for Kant and Hegel the denial of Jewish art would not have been invented." And, in spite of the fact that this notion flies in the face of the significant historical record of Jewish visual creativity dating from antiquity to the present, the concept that Jews inherently do not and cannot produce a visual culture was frequently championed by the Jews themselves. Bland lists notable modern Jewish proponents of the aniconic theory, including Bernard Berenson, Harold Rosenberg, Max Dimont, Hannah Arendt and Emmanuel Levinas. Cynthia Ozick sums up this cultural prejudice with her declaration: "Where is the Jewish Michelangelo, the Jewish Rembrandt? He has never come into being….Talented a bit, but nothing great. They never tried their hand at wood or stone or paint. 'Thou shalt have no graven images'—the Second Commandment—prevented them."

This is patently untrue historically and theologically. With few exceptions, contemporary halakhic understanding easily distinguishes between fashioning objects and images for idol worship and the creation of artworks for aesthetic edification.

Unfortunately, the historical record of rabbinic opinion has been less than reassuring, dramatically shifting primarily in relationship to external social conditions. Indeed, the range of rabbinic understandings of the Second Commandment through the ages has in fact circumscribed Jewish visual creativity and has certainly served to hamper Jews' confidence in their abilities to develop a creative visual language. That is, at least until the mid-twentieth century.

DEFINITIONS

First, let us offer some definitions that can help us clarify what we mean by "Jewish Art." For purposes of this discussion, Jewish visual art does not include Judaica and synagogue architecture simply because there is no argument about their permissibility or their extensive use throughout history.

The most parochial definition codifies Jewish Art as limited to cultural production utilizing specific Jewish subject matter, drawn from Jewish sacred and secular texts that explore Jewish social life, history and ritual. Since content is the defining factor, this can and should include artwork created by non-Jews. On the other hand, the more catholic view would include any kind of art that Jews happen to create that reference universal concepts such as peace, spirituality, brotherhood, ethnic identity, and family. Generally, these subjects simply mirror contemporary pluralistic American culture. However defined, in all its permutations it is its Jewish content that denotes the work as Jewish Art. While both formulations are important to a vital Jewish Art, important distinctions must be made in order to understand better the consequences of each approach.

Golden Age-Almost

The confluence of Postmodernism, theological diversity, and unprecedented social networking has led to a rare moment in Jewish cultural history: increased choice, clarity, and freedom in Jewish visual creativity. Hence Baigell's "Golden Age."

Just as any fledgling movement needs a history, so too does it need a vision of what will sustain its continued growth. A critical apparatus is essential for the creation of a nurturing environment of creativity. While I share Baigell's enthusiasm for the profusion of recent serious Jewish art and the enormous range of subjects explored, I simultaneously note a disheartening hesitancy to tackle a whole host of difficult but enormously fruitful Jewish subjects.

The reality is that far too many contemporary Jewish artists are content with superficial versions of Jewish ideas combined with an uncritical appropriation of contemporary art styles. And while this is not crippling to a cultural movement and may even produce a healthy diversity, in order for Jewish art to become a serious cultural expression, it must engender a creative exegesis to confront the depth and seriousness that is inherent in our rich Jewish culture.

Rabbis and Artists

Exegesis has been the rabbinic prerogative over the centuries. They are trained to be intimate with the original texts as well as with multiple commentators over the centuries. It should be obvious that a rabbinic / artistic partnership should ideally blossom every time an artist decides to create an artwork utilizing a Biblical or Jewish text. Many artists take on the task and crack open the books themselves where they can find adequate translations. Most significantly some artists have turned to contemporary rabbis to help shape and clarify their interaction with classic texts.

Siona Benjamin has worked for years with Rabbi Burton Visotzky on many of her works, especially her production of the Megillat Esther in 2011. As a noted scholar of midrash, the fertile field of rabbinic homiletical exposition, Rabbi Visotzky is uniquely poised to interact with artists. Benjamin has enlisted Rabbi Marvin Tokayer with background on Indian Jews.

For most of his career David Wander has studied with rabbis to prepare for artworks with Torah subjects. He worked with Rabbi Yonah Weinrib for his extensive series on the Book of Yonah as well as the Haggadah. Wander continues a longstanding collaboration of study with Rabbi David Kraemer adding to the impressive list of large scale accordion books created with Rabbi Kraemer including: Esther, Kohellet, Eicha, Song of Songs, Ruth, as well as narrating the stories of Noah, The Spies, David, and Judith. To be fair, many other contemporary Jewish artists are not even aware of what they are missing. The aforementioned inadequacy of Jewish education, both in terms of Judaism's texts and Jewish Art history, is appalling. Both can be remedied with sustained individual effort combined with a modern critical apparatus. I believe that it is essential to encourage Jewish artists to interrogate the very heart and soul of the *Tanakh* into their work boldly and without compunction. That is the challenge for contemporary Jewish Art.

Prospects

It should be obvious that the current revival of Jewish Art can only bloom into a true Golden Age if it has broad public support, especially from the Jewish community in America. Just as there is now a sustained readership for Jewish-oriented literature and ideas (and even occasionally some visual art) in such venues as the *Jewish Review of Books, Tablet, Jewcy,* and *The Forward,* so likewise must we develop the potentiality of a literate visual Jewish culture and audience.

Jewish institutions across the board, including synagogues, community centers, museums and media, must raise the bar and demand textual literacy. A constant daily outpouring of Jewish texts, in English and Hebrew, must inundate our communities. Our writers must not dumb down complex Jewish concepts; rather, we must have confidence that our people will always be curious to find out more about their precious heritage. Equally important is community education in visual literacy; our community should insist upon being visually literate in the two-thousand years of Jewish Art in both the Jewish and Western visual canon.

Critics and journalists must be encouraged to analyze, thoughtfully comment on, and explain these artists' works to a Jewish audience so that both the Judaic and aesthetic elements are treated with equal respect. The public must listen and become engaged. The Jewish museums must overcome their reluctance and open their doors. In order to thrive, the Golden Age must be recognized.

We have made a good start. From out of the wilderness of our own doubts, we have found our way through a troubled past and, thanks to America's loving embrace, we have emerged into a new artistic landscape full of promise. More artists, self-consciously drawing upon Jewish Tradition as a springboard for inspiration, have produced more explicitly Jewish Art. If we can muster the courage to stand apart as proud Jews in contemporary America, while fully embracing three-thousand years of our history and close to two-thousand years of visual creativity, contemporary Jewish Art has more than a fair chance to find its rightful day in the sun.

SHEMOT
CREATIVITY AND SUFFERING: CONFRONTATION WITH NON-BEING

In Egypt, the Jewish people grew into a national entity, increasing in numbers, wealth and prominence. The Torah states (Shemot 1:7):

7. The children of Israel were fruitful and swarmed and increased and became very, very strong, and the land became filled with them.	ז. וּבְנֵי יִשְׂרָאֵל פָּרוּ וַיִּשְׁרְצוּ וַיִּרְבּוּ וַיַּעַצְמוּ בִּמְאֹד מְאֹד וַתִּמָּלֵא הָאָרֶץ אֹתָם:
Rashi: and swarmed: They bore six children at each birth.	וישרצו: שהיו יולדות ששה בכרס אחד:

The Passover Hagaddah clarifies the phrase "and became there a nation", in this verse, stating: "And he became there a nation". This teaches that Israel was distinctive there." This unprecedented increase of the size of the Jewish population and the distinctive, separate quality of Jewish life from the other Egyptians (language, dress, food and, of course, religion), brought fear to Pharaoh and his advisors that a "fifth column" of potential traitors or revolutionaries might be in their midst. In the Torah, Pharaoh" states:

10. Get ready, let us deal shrewdly with them, lest they increase, and a war befall us, and they join our enemies and depart from the land.	יְהָבָה נִתְחַכְּמָה לוֹ פֶּן יִרְבֶּה וְהָיָה כִּי תִקְרֶאנָה מִלְחָמָה וְנוֹסַף גַּם הוּא עַל שֹׂנְאֵינוּ וְנִלְחַם בָּנוּ וְעָלָה מִן הָאָרֶץ:

The Egyptian political system was one of coercion. It was a slave society even before the Jewish people were enslaved. But it suited the Egyptians to have the Jews carry out other roles in the society. When the Jewish people's size and distinctiveness "tipped the balance" and it was surmised by the Egyptian leaders that this valuable commodity might simply vacate Egypt and take their talents and labor with them, they were reassigned as a slave class. One could surmise that Egypt was experienced at the process of enslavement and enacted these edicts over time, with the Jewish people acquiescing so as not to engender further wrath of the authorities. Similar processes took place during the Jewish Diaspora, throughout Medieval, Renaissance and pre-enlightenment Europe as well as in many Arab countries, continuing up to recent times. This process of course took its most ghastly form in Nazi Germany and the areas the Reich controlled.

In the case of the Egyptian persecution, the more the Jewish people were abused, the more they increased in number.

2. But as much as they would afflict them, so did they multiply and so did they gain strength, and they were disgusted because of the children of Israel.	יב. וְכַאֲשֶׁר יְעַנּוּ אֹתוֹ כֵּן יִרְבֶּה וְכֵן יִפְרֹץ וַיָּקֻצוּ מִפְּנֵי בְּנֵי יִשְׂרָאֵל:

This unexplainable population explosion led to greater fear by the Egyptians and greater persecutions, until families were separated, harsh enslavement imposed and male children were collected by the Egyptian populous and drowned in the river. (Shemot 1:13,14 and 22)

13. So the Egyptians enslaved the children of Israel with back-breaking labor.	יג. וַיַּעֲבִדוּ מִצְרַיִם אֶת בְּנֵי יִשְׂרָאֵל בְּפָרֶךְ:
14. And they embittered their lives with hard labor, with clay and with bricks and with all kinds of labor in the fields, all	יד. וַיְמָרֲרוּ אֶת חַיֵּיהֶם בַּעֲבֹדָה קָשָׁה בְּחֹמֶר וּבִלְבֵנִים וּבְכָל עֲבֹדָה בַּשָּׂדֶה אֵת כָּל עֲבֹדָתָם

their work that they worked with them with back breaking labor.	אֲשֶׁר עָבְדוּ בָהֶם בְּפָרֶךְ:
22. And Pharaoh commanded all his people, saying, "Every son who is born you shall cast into the Nile, and every daughter you shall allow to live."	כב. וַיְצַו פַּרְעֹה לְכָל עַמּוֹ לֵאמֹר כָּל הַבֵּן הַיִּלּוֹד הַיְאֹרָה תַּשְׁלִיכֻהוּ וְכָל הַבַּת תְּחַיּוּן:

It seems to me that there is a deep parallel between Pharaoh's reaction to the Jewish people and that of Hitler. Both reacted with murderous cruelty towards the Jews out of fear and a sense of the Jewish people uniqueness and impact. In spite of Hitler's diatribes regarding the Jewish people as vermin and an inferior race, it is obvious that he feared their power on some level. In his fantasies of the Jews as the cause of Germany's defeat in World War I and his attributing to them the power to "foul" the Aryan race, he clearly displays an immense terror at their unique capabilities. This attitude is shared by Pharaoh as well, where he states in this same chapter:

9. He said to his people, "Behold, the people of the children of Israel are more numerous and stronger than we are."	ט. וַיֹּאמֶר אֶל עַמּוֹ הִנֵּה עַם בְּנֵי יִשְׂרָאֵל רַב וְעָצוּם מִמֶּנּוּ:

I don't believe that this is a literal statement-that the Jews were more numerous and powerful than the Egyptian people and their army. But there is clarity on Pharaoh's part that the Jews have a strength that cannot be defeated. Perhaps it is a sense possessed of every person, whose soul communicates with the Creator on a conscious or pre-conscious level, that the Jews are a people of God and are, essentially, an undefeatable divine force, in spite of their apparent weaknesses and the persecutions and degradations that they have endured throughout their long history. This sometimes seems to me to be the reason behind the outsized interest and emotional unease that many nations of the world have regarding the might that the State of Israel possesses in the present day.

As the verse says, "they (the Egyptians) were disgusted because of the children of Israel":

2. But as much as they would afflict them, so did they multiply and so did they gain strength, and they were disgusted because of the children of Israel.	יב. וְכַאֲשֶׁר יְעַנּוּ אֹתוֹ כֵּן יִרְבֶּה וְכֵן יִפְרֹץ וַיָּקֻצוּ מִפְּנֵי בְּנֵי יִשְׂרָאֵל:

The success of the Jewish people of Modern Israel "disgusts" many in the world who may sense in it as an indication of their unique, exalted role. Esau and Ishmael (portrayed by Jewish tradition as the root of Christianity and Islam) have not forgiven the loss of the mantle of leadership from the family of Abraham. As long as Israel remained an exiled, pathetic people, the brother nation's ire was contained. Also, Esau and Ishmael had the pleasure of abusing the powerless Jews on many occasions to further prove to themselves that the Jews could not be the chosen of God. But with the State of Israel, the psycho-dynamic changed and the fight over who is the chosen one was revitalized. I know this perspective may seem chauvinistic and far-fetched since Modern Israel is, for the most part, a secular state and European Christianity is currently highly secular in its perspective. However, all souls communicate on a deep level with God and the battle for and against God's will is an ongoing one in each person, whether they characterize it as such or not. For many children of Esau and Ishmael, The Modern State of Israel must be destroyed to restore their sense of equilibrium and remove the "disgust" from their lives, in a similar way that the Egyptians could not stand the prominence of the Jews in their midst.

Suffering in the Jewish People's History

Due to the Jewish people's uncanny ability to succeed in worldly, scholarly and artistic affairs, recent times have seen the Jewish people rise to heights of leadership in all areas of scholarship, arts and sciences. The Jews have also become prosperous in modern times. The establishment of the State of Israel and its ascent as a modern, technological and military state in a matter of decades, is another enormous source of pride and victory for the Jewish people. There is no parallel for this situation during the Diaspora. For a Jew, pride is a natural response to the astounding successes that Jewish people have accomplished in every field. In America we as Jews are safer, freer, more prosperous and more productive than at any time of our recent history. But this state is an exceptional one during our two thousand year exile. It has not always been this way.

The Jewish nation was born in suffering and, by most accounts, has endured more suffering than any other nation. Every human torment and degradation has been heaped upon the Jew, to the point that many have joked that, it is true that the Jews are the chosen people, but the question is "chosen for what?" Suffering, even if we do not experience it on a national level, during the present time, is always close to the Jewish person's heart. As we are reminded at the Passover Seder in the Haggadah:

> For not just one alone has risen against us to destroy us, but in every generation they rise against us to destroy us;

and the Holy One, blessed be He, saves us from their hand!

Every year on Tasha Brave we lament and relive the experience of the horrific destruction of the first Temple, and the starvation and murder that accompanied it. We are still living in the long shadow of the Holocaust and the grotesque slaughter of six million of our people. We now have a Jewish nation that lives in a siege state surrounding by a billion Arabs who pray and plot its destruction daily. Yes, we are a people experienced with suffering. When we are not suffering we imagine the potential of suffering in our own and the lives of others. Perhaps this explains why Jews find suffering in anyone so intolerable and why we have been leaders in all areas of endeavor that seek to help those who are suffering, to find relief and liberation.

What is Suffering and Why it is Uniquely Human?

Why is suffering, as they say, "good for the soul"? Is suffering something to be sought? Certainly not. One would be emotionally ill to seek suffering out. But if suffering comes upon a person, the question is whether it can it be a beneficial experience that helps the sufferer grow and be able to experience life in a more meaningful, fulfilling way? Rabbi Joseph B. Soloveitchik ("the Rav") has written extensive on the subject of suffering. Many of these writings have been collected in the text "Out of the Whirlwind: Essays on Mourning, Suffering and the Human Condition". We will draw heavily from this text in our further exploration of what suffering is, and its role in the development of the person. To begin with, suffering is to be understood as a uniquely human activity and not one that is shared by animals. The Rav distinguishes between suffering and pain. He states:

> We must distinguish between pain and suffering. While pain is a physico-psychical sensation and is proper not only in humans but even to the animals, suffering is a spiritual experience which is characteristic of man alone. A mother in labor who fervently beseeches God to give her a child cannot forego the sensation of excruciating pain. But she is not a woman of sorrow; on the contrary, she is a happy woman whose most cherished dream comes true. On the other hand, one who suddenly discovers that he is afflicted with a fatal disease and is doomed, even though he is free from pain, is a man of suffering and his distress is overwhelming. (p. 123)

The Rav explains in this essay that the suffering of man has its root in one of two horrific realizations, both of which result from a person's awareness of his non-being or non-existence on some level. The two sources of this realization are: 1-when man is confronted with his death in a manner that he cannot deny or push away, and 2: when man is confronted with his having, through his acts or circumstance, forfeited the sense he has of his worth and value. In both these cases, the person is confronted with his being a "nothing" or "non-being" and he suffers. The expression "suffering is good for the soul" has an unanticipated level of accuracy, as suffering, according to the Rav, takes place in and only in, the soul. The Rav states:

> This meeting with nihility may take place in two ways. First, it occurs when the individual existence is threatened with extinction. The anticipation and fear of death is a singular trait of man alone, who was endowed with a strange time consciousness which runs out bit by bit, driving him gradually to his destiny-nihility. Second, it takes place at the axiological level. The existential experience is an awareness of something which not only is but is worthy of its unique form of existence. In other words, man not only exists as a spiritual being but also values his existence as precious. His existence is not a static factum but an actus committed to something which fascinates him…Man is charged with a task; this feeling of responsibility is part of his existential

awareness. Of course, the objectives of his responsible questing and the ways in which he tries to attain them vary. Yet man is a being committed to an idea, even though quite often this idea may be false, absurd and perverted-and the means of achievement degrading. Whenever man realizes that he has failed to fulfill his commitment or responsibility, thus forfeiting the worth of his existence, he turns into a man of affliction. (pgs 123-124)

Suffering Makes the Man

Rabbi Solovetichik's elucidation of suffering continues with his insight into the role of suffering-specifically the encounter with non-being- and how it and only it can raise the person's life to a new level of meaningfulness, depth and joy. As a person passes from the simple natural state of goals and pursuits of pleasure, power and mastery (termed by the Rav as "cosmic man") to one who has encountered the awe, terror of and submission to God (termed by the Rav as "covenantal man") a new world opens up to him. He states:

> First, there is a moment of shock, when finite man, upon being confronted with infinity, becomes aware of the ontic void, of the inner contradiction within his existential experience, and suddenly realizes that the very foundation of his existence has collapsed. In other words, man in his rendezvous with God is confronted by non-being, by nihility, since God, addressing Himself through apocalypse, negates any other existence. Second, there is the moment of ecstasy and rapture which rehabilitates and reconstructs man to heights unattainable at a cosmic level. Meeting God is a glorious and the most blessed event; it helps man transcend himself and makes him greater than he really is. Man becomes transported out of himself and suddenly awakens to new dimensions of reality that were alien to him before. Communion with God elevates the spirit, cleanses the heart and spurs on the mind to absurd greatness…The rendezvous with the God dwelling within being brings the ideal of self-realization within his reach. (p. 121)

The Rav provides a recounting of his own personal meeting with non-being and how it brought him terror and a destruction of the ego, followed by a new level of clarity and truer sense of his own existence. He states:

> The night preceding my operation I prayed to God and beseeched Him to spare me. I did not ask for too much. All I wanted was that He should make it possible for me to attend my daughter's wedding, which was postponed on account of my illness-a very modest wish in comparison with my insane claims to life prior to my sickness. The fantastic flights of human foolishness and egocentrism were distant from me that night. However, this "fall" from the heights of an illusory immortality into the valley of finitude was the greatest achievement of the long hours of anxiety and uncertainty. Fundamentally, this change was not an act of falling but one of rising toward a new existential awareness which embraces both man's tragedy and his glory, in all its ambivalence and paradoxality. I stopped perceiving myself in categories of eternity. (p. 131)

The Rav continues, explaining that the paradigmatic shift of one's sense of self from infinite to finite, which is brought on by the personal confrontation of death, transforms all the varied assessments of one's life that are now seen on the finite plane as opposed to the illusionary infinite one. He explains:

> When one's perspective is shifted from the illusion of eternity to the reality of temporality, one finds peace of mind and relief from other worries, from his petty fears and from absurd stresses and nonsensical nightmares. At the level of the antithetic existential experience, man extracts himself from the throng of ghosts which keep on haunting him. At the root of our restlessness lies a distorted conception of ourselves as immortal beings. Hence, everything that causes pain or annoyance is placed in the wrong frame of reference. We foolishly imagine eternity to be affected by a particular event which disturbed us; we magnify the significance of incidents because we exaggerate our own worth. Man sees himself in the mirror of immortality. Hence his desires, dreams, ambitions and visions assume absolute significance, and any frustrating experience may break man. When one frees himself from

this obsession, his perspective becomes coherent and his suffering bearable. (p. 132)

The Message of Suffering

Rabbi Soloveitchik implores us not to repress or push away the suffering experiences that we go through in an attempt to return to our former state of non-awareness of the antithetical nature of existence. There is, of course, a great temptation to return to the illusory bliss of our own personal immortality and infinite value. This would be a great "waste of the suffering" we have endured. The Rav states:

> For the risk is great that man, driven by his innate tendency to immerse in spiritual joys, to keep away from himself the memory of any unpleasant sensation, to repress disturbing thoughts and to escape from a past that abounds in sorrow, will let the catastrophic event drift aimlessly in a vacuum without finding anchorage in the total personal experience. This would amount to wasting the catastrophic disclosure, to an admission that God was absent from the whirlwind that thwarts man's drives and dreams. In consequence, man would, after meeting God in the whirlwind, return to his routine which operates exclusively at the level of affirmation, refusing stubbornly to relate itself to negation. (pgs. 140-141)

Intuitive Knowledge's Impact on the Scholar and Artist

In this same group of essays in the text "Out of the Whirlwind", Rabbi Soloveitchik makes clear that creative Torah scholarship, which is at the center of the Jewish worldview consists of two different levels of creative thought. One, which he describes as the "halakhik logos and ethos" focuses on creative categorical thinking utilized to clarify the nature of the law and translate it into the covenant's normative structure which defines and guides one's will and action. The Rav states:

> It is not enough to do; it is also important and essential to understand, to know. Basically the positive Halakhah lays claim to the mind of man and to his will-will translated into action; not just the abstract decision in the Kantian fashion, but the decision which is later translated and transformed into deed. (p. 87).

The second level of creativity in Torah scholarship is one that is focused on the intuitive sense, an inner quality by which ones lives within a God-infused existence. The Rav states:

> The dominant matter of this second gesture on the part of Halakhah-not the positive conceptual gesture but the axiological gesture-is not *"ve-nishma" ("and we will understand")* but *"Ta'anu u-re'u ki tov Hashem, Taste and see that the Lord is good"* (Ps. 34:9)....It means that God can be tasted, beheld intuitively, confronted and related to. Man can share in God." (p. 89)

It is this second level of creativity that is profoundly impacted by the suffering experience and the encounter with God that potentially comes in its wake. For the artist, like the scholar, the encounter with suffering and the realization of the antithetical nature of existence (surging forward coupled with accepting defeat and reversal) creates an enlightened persona and impacts the perspective and inspiration for the creative act. The artist is transformed and raised to a higher level of clarity, resulting in art that embraces this reality and communicates it through varied mediums and methods.

The Primacy of Service for the Scholar and the Artist

The Rav explains that when a person moves through a suffering experience that results in the disillusioning, redeeming encounter with God, his life is transformed to one in which service takes a central role. The Rav states:

> When we experience the swing back from an illusory eternity to a temporal reality, a new category is discovered, namely that of service. God summons us to His service; we are called upon to serve Him. We are appointed as the servants of God….There can be no religious experience if it does not entail the element of service. Our existence is not just a coincidence, a mechanical fact, a meaningless caprice on the part of nature or providence, but a meaningful assignment which abounds in responsibility and commitment….Judaism believe that every individual is capable of qualifying himself for Divine service. Rich and poor, genius and simpleton, master and slave-they are fit to serve God in some capacity. Every person possesses something unique, by virtue of which he differs from the thou, making him or her irreplaceable and indispensable-the inner worth of a one-timely, unique, never-to-be duplicated existence, which can and must serve God by self-involvement in the drama of redemption at all levels.
> (p. 148)

By recognizing one's mortality and finite existence the creative work of the scholar or the artist is transformed from the mere expression of inner feeling or perspectives into an act of service to God through which the specific talents he or she uniquely possesses participates in the great redemptive drama of the world. As the Rav explains:

> If one lives in an illusory eternity, he may miss the call; he may not hear the voice which addresses itself to him; he may not realize that God Himself turns to him and summons him to His service…Yet if the time awareness is awakened in me, if I suddenly become cognizant of an existence which has been withdrawn from the realm of my influence, where I convert the present moment into creative performance, potentiality into an event and time into service, I realize that I have missed the call, that I am late for the execution of my task, for the fulfillment of my mission. I also begin to comprehend the responsibility which my time-experience entails, the norm of vigilance and alertness every moment, since the call comes through often, at very short intervals. I anticipate the future with trepidation and anxiety, because it is the time in which I

may act and serve. Every fraction of the infinite stream of time becomes precious. (pp. 148-149)

POETRY ON THE PARSHA

Nelly Sachs was born in Berlin in 1891 and escaped Nazi Germany to Stockholm in 1940. She received the Nobel Prize for Literature in 1966 and died in 1970 (translated from German by Harry Zohn).

Chorus of the Rescued by Nelly Sachs

We the rescued, out of whose hollow bones Death was already carving its flutes,
Across whose sinews Death was already moving its bow-
The mourning of our bodies still resound with their maimed music.
We the rescued, still see the nooses twisted for our necks hanging in the blue air.
The hour glasses are still filling with our dripping blood.
We the rescued, are still gnawed at by the worms of fear.
Our stars are buried in the dust.
We, the rescued, beg of you: Show us our sun slowly,
Lead us from star to star step by step.
Gently let us learn to live again.
Otherwise, the song of a bird, the filling of a pail at the well
Could tear open again badly sealed pain and flush us away.
We beg you: do not show us a barking dog as yet.
It could be, it just could be that we shall disintegrate into dust,
Turn into dust before your eyes.
For what keeps our substance together?
We have become devoid of breath since our souls fled to Him in the dark of night,
Long before they rescued our bodies.
We, the rescued, press your hands, recognize your eyes-

But what keeps us together is only the parting;
The parting in the dust is what connects us with you.

The following poem is by Paul Celan. During World War 2, his parents were sent to an extermination camp and Celan to a labor camp. He settled in Paris in 1948 and died in 1970. "Death Fugue" is, perhaps his most famous poem.

Death Fugue by Paul Celan

Black milk of dawn we drink it at dusk
we drink it at noon and at daybreak we drink it at night
we drink it and drink it
we are digging a grave in the air there's room for us all
a man lives in the house he plays with the serpents he writes
he writes when its darkens to Germany your golden hair Margarete
he writes it and steps outside and the stars all aglisten he whistles for his hounds
he whistles for his Jews he has them dig a grave in the earth
he commands us to play for the dance

Black milk of dawn we drink it at dusk
we drink it at noon and at daybreak we drink it at night
we drink it and drink it
we are digging a grave in the air there's room for us all
a man lives in the house he plays with the serpents he writes
he writes when its darkens to Germany your golden hair Margarete
your ashen hair Shulamite we are digging a grave in the air there's room for us all

He shouts cut deeper in the earth to some the rest of you sing and play
He reaches for the iron in his belt he heaves it his eyes are blue

Make your spades cut deeper the rest of you play for the dance

Black milk of dawn we drink it at dusk
we drink it at noon and at daybreak we drink it at night
we drink it and drink it
we are digging a grave in the air there's room for us all
a man lives in the house he plays with the serpents he writes
he writes when its darkens to Germany your golden hair Margarete
 your ashen hair Shulamite he plays with the serpents

He shouts play death more sweetly death is a master from Germany
he shouts play the violins darker you'll rise as smoke in the air
then you'll have a grave in the clouds there's room for you all

Black milk of dawn we drink you at night
we drink you at noon death is a master from Germany

PAINTINGS ON THE PARSHA

The Encounter with Suffering

Moses, raised in the Egyptian royal household, first encountered Jewish suffering when he went out and witnessed an Egyptian taskmaster beating a Jewish slave. His reaction was swift, promptly murdering the Egyptian and burying him in the sand. It is more than a little shocking to see Moses, the consummate lawgiver, summarily executing another human being. This violent encounter must have left a deep scar on Moses' personality. (R.M.)

Moses Kills the Egyptian by Richard McBee

Informing the other half of the suffering equation, a similar kind of violence is now directed at Moses himself. As Moses was returning to Egypt at God's command, he was suddenly attacked by God Himself on the way. Only Zipporah's insightful and quick action in circumcising their son saved Moses' life. The lessons of Jewish suffering; those committed by Jews and non-Jews and those committed by God, creates an existential anxiety through which we must navigate a halakchic and meaningful life. (R.M.)

God Attacks Moses by Richard McBee

VAERA
CREATIVITY, MIRACLES AND THE SENSES IN RELIGIOUS EXPERIENCE

In the *parsha* of Vaera we behold the beginning of the redemption the Jewish people from Egyptian bondage. God accomplishes this deliverance with a dazzling display of *makkot* (plagues), seven of which are described in this week's Torah reading. These seven are 1) turning of the Nile River to blood; 2) bringing of countless frogs (or crocodiles) to invade every nook and cranny of Egypt; 3) bringing of the plague of lice, causing intense itching and discomfort; 4) invasion of Egypt by the wild beasts of the field and jungle causing widespread injury and destruction; 5) killing of the Egyptians domestic animals with disease; 6) bringing of a disease of boils to the Egyptians; 7) raining of large flaming hailstones from the atmosphere, destroying people and property. All of these plagues occurred throughout Egypt, with the exception of the area of Goshen where the Jewish people lived. Never before in human history had God revealed Himself in such a public, unequivocal display. The *makkot* made clear the distinct quality of the Jewish people as having a specific role guided by God's providential care. God informs Moshe in Shemot 6:6-7:

| 6. Therefore, say to the children of Israel, 'I am the Lord, and I will take you out from under the burdens of the Egyptians, and I will save you from their labor, and I will redeem you with an outstretched arm and with great judgments. | ו. לָכֵן אֱמֹר לִבְנֵי יִשְׂרָאֵל אֲנִי יְהוָה וְהוֹצֵאתִי אֶתְכֶם מִתַּחַת סִבְלֹת מִצְרַיִם וְהִצַּלְתִּי אֶתְכֶם מֵעֲבֹדָתָם וְגָאַלְתִּי אֶתְכֶם בִּזְרוֹעַ נְטוּיָה וּבִשְׁפָטִים גְּדֹלִים: |

> 7. And I will take you to Me as a people, and I will be a God to you, and you will know that I am the Lord your God, Who has brought you out from under the burdens of the Egyptians.
>
> ז. וְלָקַחְתִּי אֶתְכֶם לִי לְעָם וְהָיִיתִי לָכֶם לֵאלֹהִים וִידַעְתֶּם כִּי אֲנִי יְהוָה אֱלֹהֵיכֶם הַמּוֹצִיא אֶתְכֶם מִתַּחַת סִבְלוֹת מִצְרָיִם:

God also informs Moshe that through this redemption Egypt will know of God and his mastery of the world of nature and of history. God states:

> And the Egyptians shall know that I am the Lord when I stretch forth My hand over Egypt, and I will take the children of Israel out of their midst.
>
> ה. וְיָדְעוּ מִצְרַיִם כִּי אֲנִי יְהוָה בִּנְטֹתִי אֶת יָדִי עַל מִצְרָיִם וְהוֹצֵאתִי אֶת בְּנֵי יִשְׂרָאֵל מִתּוֹכָם:
>
> (Shemot 7:5)

Redemption from Egypt and Direct Sensual Experience

Judaism is a cerebral religion at its core. Its most prized activity is study of the Torah and the most exalted of our heroes are people whose focus is wisdom and a deep subtle understanding. Moshe is *"Moshe Rebbenu"* ("Moses our teacher"). According to Maimonides, God communicates with man, primarily through intellectual experience. Prophecy occurs within the mental landscape, in a dream or vision. Maimonides states in the "Guide for the Perplexed":

> In *Beresheit Rabba* (section xvii) the following saying of our sages occurs, "Dream is the *nobelet* (the unripe fruit) of prophecy". This is an excellent comparison, for the unripe fruit (*nobelet*) is really the fruit to some extent, only it has fallen from the tree before it was fully developed and ripe. In a similar manner the action of the imaginative faculty during sleep is the same as at the time when it receives a

> prophecy, only in the first case it is not fully developed, and has not yet reached its highest degree. But why need I quote the words of our Sages, when I can refer to the following passage of Scripture: "If there be among you a prophet, I, the Lord, will make myself known unto him in a vision, in a dream will I speak to him" (Num. xii. 6). Here the Lord tells us what the real essence of prophecy is, that it is a perfection acquired in a dream or in a vision; the imaginative faculty acquires such an efficiency in its action that it sees the thing as if it came from without, and perceives it as if through the medium of bodily senses. These two modes of prophecy, vision and dream, include all its different degrees. (Book 2, Chapter 36).

The Rambam also holds that human contact with *malachim* ("angels of God") are experienced within the mind as well, and not in the spatial-temporal world.   He states:

> We have already stated that the forms in which angels appear form part of the prophetic vision. Some prophets see angels in the form of man, e.g., "And behold three men stood by him" (Gen. xviii.2); others perceive an angel as a fearful and terrible being, e.g., "And his countenance was as the countenance of an angel of God, very terrible" (Judges xiii. 6) ; others see them as fire, e.g., "And the angel of the Lord appeared to him in a flame of fire" (Exod. Iii. 2). In *Beresheit Rabba* (chap. 1.) the following remark occurs: "To Abraham, whose prophetic power was great, they appeared in the form of men; to Lot, whose power was weak, they appeared as angels." This is an important principle as regards prophecy…every appearance of an angel is part of a prophetic vision, depending on the capacity of the person that perceives it. (Book 2: Chapter 6)

But with regards to the redemption from Egypt and the public miracles that took place at that time, these are not considered by Maimonides or any of the other sages of our tradition as a vision of the mind or a subtle change in nature that impact historic outcomes in some hidden way. The redemption from Egypt was, on the contrary, a most dazzling experience of the senses through which people saw, heard, smelled, tasted and felt the presence and will of God within the world of time and space. To deny the actual taking place of the miracles of the redemption is fundamentally contrary to Jewish law and tradition.

One may ask the question – why was such a bold miraculous display necessary? There is an understanding among our scholars that God does not "favor" open miracles and that it constitutes, in a sense, a disturbance of the perfectly created order of the universe with its constant laws. Rabbi Soloveitchik, in his essay "And From There You Shall Seek Him" ("*U'vkashtem Mesham*") states:

> Judaism does not pursue miracles that occur outside the realm of nature, which have such an important place in the thought of the universal *homo religiosus*. The Jewish sages were uncomfortable about altering the natural way of things. In the Jewish view, miracles and wonders occur only when absolutely necessary, when all other means have been exhausted and man is attacked by his enemies in a place from which he cannot escape. Using a shortcut in the natural realm (even in this case) does not add any glory to the splendor that shines forth from ordered, law-governed reality. On the contrary, it mars the honor of the Creator. The leap from lawful to miraculous revelation is described by the Midrash as a descent, as a degradation of the *Shekhinah* (see *Exodus Rabbah* 15:5). Only because of His great goodness and lovingkindness does God "defile" Himself in order to save His chosen people or punish the wicked. The orderly creation, characterized by monochromatic lawfulness, tells the greatness of God....Consciousness of Him does not require interruptions of the causal regime. (p. 133)

In light of this perspective, wasn't it possible for God to "arrange" the redemption of the Jewish people and the punishment of the Egyptians in a subtle, hidden manner as was done in the time of Purim, where we note that the name of God is completely absent from Megillah of Esther and the miracles were accomplished in a manner by which God's hand arranged fortuitous occurrences that combined to turn a devastating destruction into a tremendous victory. What then was the purpose of the bold miracles performed for all to see in Egypt and to be awed by? This impact was certainly the intention. As we learn that in the later plagues, Pharaoh's "heart was hardened" by God to assure that the full display of miracles would take place. The Torah states:

11. And the necromancers could not stand before Moses because of the boils, for the boils were upon the necromancers and upon all Egypt.	יא. וְלֹא יָכְלוּ הַחַרְטֻמִּים לַעֲמֹד לִפְנֵי מֹשֶׁה מִפְּנֵי הַשְּׁחִין כִּי הָיָה הַשְּׁחִין בַּחֲרְטֻמִּם וּבְכָל מִצְרָיִם:
12. But the Lord strengthened Pharaoh's heart, and he did not hearken to them, as the Lord spoke to Moses.	יב. וַיְחַזֵּק יְהֹוָה אֶת לֵב פַּרְעֹה וְלֹא שָׁמַע אֲלֵהֶם כַּאֲשֶׁר דִּבֶּר יְהֹוָה אֶל מֹשֶׁה:

(Shemot 7:11-12)

It seems from this statement of the Torah that the redemption could have been carried out with fewer miracles had Pharaoh been allowed to act on his terror and release the Jewish people. What was the need for the full display of miraculous *makkot* ("plagues") that took place during the redemption? Perhaps they were needed to bolster the esteem of the Jewish people and make them realize that God has truly chosen them for a divine mission on Earth? Was it done for the sake of the Egyptians, so that they would be given an opportunity to see the glory of God which they could understand? Was it done for the generations of Jews to come as they are enjoined to consider themselves at the seder, as if they themselves were redeemed from the slavery of Egypt? Let us briefly explore these possibilities.

The Need for A Dazzling Display Due to the Immaturity and Exhausted Nature of the Audience

In Egypt you had two main "audiences" for this dazzling show of God's mastery over nature and His care and concern for the Jewish people. The audiences were the Jewish people themselves, and the Egyptian people (including Pharaoh). I would like to suggest that both of these audiences were disadvantaged in their ability to understand a more subtle display of God's providence and rule. The Jewish people had degenerated due to their involvement in Egyptian society, with its lasciviousness and idolatry. The Egyptians glorified in grand physical display (e.g.- the pyramids) and indulged in a gross sensual lifestyle. The extent to which the Jews partook of this lifestyle and descended to what our sages described as "the 49th level of *tumah*" (uncleanness- of which there are only 50 levels) expresses this profound degeneration. Also, the Torah tells us, that the Jewish people's spirit was exhausted by the hardships of slavery and oppression, which prevented them from following Moshe at their first meeting. The Torah states (Shemot 6:9):

| 9. Moses spoke thus to the children of Israel, but they did not hearken to Moses because of [their] shortness of breath and because of [their] hard labor. | ט. וַיְדַבֵּר מֹשֶׁה כֵּן אֶל בְּנֵי יִשְׂרָאֵל וְלֹא שָׁמְעוּ אֶל מֹשֶׁה מִקֹּצֶר רוּחַ וּמֵעֲבֹדָה קָשָׁה: |

The Egyptians were hampered in their ability to notice more subtle displays of God's providence due to this sensuous lifestyle. With regards to impacting the Egyptians through the plagues, the Torah is quite clear. It states:

3. But I will harden Pharaoh's heart, and I will increase My signs and My wonders in the land of Egypt.	ג. וַאֲנִי אַקְשֶׁה אֶת לֵב פַּרְעֹה וְהִרְבֵּיתִי אֶת אֹתֹתַי וְאֶת מוֹפְתַי בְּאֶרֶץ מִצְרָיִם:
4. But Pharaoh will not hearken to you, and I will lay My hand upon the Egyptians, and I will take My legions, My people, the children of Israel, out of Egypt with great judgments.	ד. וְלֹא יִשְׁמַע אֲלֵכֶם פַּרְעֹה וְנָתַתִּי אֶת יָדִי בְּמִצְרָיִם וְהוֹצֵאתִי אֶת צִבְאֹתַי אֶת עַמִּי בְנֵי יִשְׂרָאֵל מֵאֶרֶץ מִצְרַיִם בִּשְׁפָטִים גְּדֹלִים:
5. And the Egyptians shall know that I am the Lord when I stretch forth My hand over Egypt, and I will take the children of Israel out of their midst.	ה. וְיָדְעוּ מִצְרַיִם כִּי אֲנִי יְהֹוָה בִּנְטֹתִי אֶת יָדִי עַל מִצְרָיִם וְהוֹצֵאתִי אֶת בְּנֵי יִשְׂרָאֵל מִתּוֹכָם:

(Shemot 7: 3-5)

When you are dealing with people that are immature, sated, and at a low level of appreciating subtlety and sensitivity in their perception and understanding due to exhaustion or an over-stimulated, sensual lifestyle. They need to be addressed on their level in order to make an impression on them. We see this in a number of modern-day situations. Most of the stunning blockbuster Broadway shows and movies use dazzling special effects to tell a story and entertain an audience that has become accustomed to crass, visual displays in today's ubiquitous media barrage. The telling of a subtle, sensitive story is becoming less and less common. Also, when dealing with an immature audience such as children, visual effects, colors and movement are important to maintain the child's attention and create a sense of wonder and excitement. In Egypt, God had to produce a show that would "play well" to a sated, degenerate audience and, for the

Jews, one that was also exhausted and had no patience to search for subtle meaning and hints in a plot. Thus the miracles! The mother of all special effects!

It was only through the bold display of ten miraculous events that profoundly impacted the lifestyle and senses of the people that this particular audience would be able to take note of God and his message would result in the idea leaving a lasting impression. The miracles were performed as much for the Egyptians as they were for the Jewish people. Egypt was given its chance to learn of God's existence and His providential relationship with history. Right then and there they could have become another people of God resulting in a history of mankind that would have taken a completely different form. The mercy of the miracles is that God "lowered" His glory by interrupting the perfect order of His creation to provide the Jewish people and the Egyptians with a revelation that they, in their low state, could note and understand.

Redemption from Egypt: Playing at a Seder Near You!

The miracles of Egypt happened only once in history. But we are enjoined to retell, relive and reimagine the story each year at the Passover seder. There is a Torah commandment to tell your children of these events "*hegadtah l-vinckha*"- as the Torah states:

20. If your son asks you in time to come, saying, "What are the testimonies, the statutes, and the ordinances, which the Lord our God has commanded you?"	כ. כִּי יִשְׁאָלְךָ בִנְךָ מָחָר לֵאמֹר מָה הָעֵדֹת וְהַחֻקִּים וְהַמִּשְׁפָּטִים אֲשֶׁר צִוָּה יְהוָה אֱלֹהֵינוּ אֶתְכֶם:

21. You shall say to your son, "We were slaves to Pharaoh in Egypt, and the Lord took us out of Egypt with a strong hand.	כא. וְאָמַרְתָּ לְבִנְךָ עֲבָדִים הָיִינוּ לְפַרְעֹה בְּמִצְרָיִם וַיּוֹצִיאֵנוּ יְהֹוָה מִמִּצְרַיִם בְּיָד חֲזָקָה:
22. And the Lord gave signs and wonders, great and terrible, upon Egypt, upon Pharaoh, and upon all his household, before our eyes.	כב. וַיִּתֵּן יְהֹוָה אוֹתֹת וּמֹפְתִים גְּדֹלִים וְרָעִים בְּמִצְרַיִם בְּפַרְעֹה וּבְכָל בֵּיתוֹ לְעֵינֵינוּ:

But we do more than simply retell the story. We create a multi-sense event in which the child hears, sees, tastes and smells the events of the redemption throughout the activities of the seder evening. We, as adults, are also enjoined to consider and imagine ourselves as if we were redeemed on that night. In Rabbi Serkin's collection of Rabbi Soloveitchik's lectures (*shiurim*), "*Hararey Kedem*", it is stated in the name of Rabbi Soloveitchik:

> …the form and character of the recounting is to be done such that we enter with all our strength into the story and the mitzvah is to tell all the details with full emotion until it seem on account of this telling that one feels as if he went out of Egypt. This is the recounting "into" the redemption from Egypt - specifically to be completely immersed in the body of the story, since this recounting is a "fulfillment of the heart (*kiyam b'lav*) and one is obligated to be completely absorbed in the story. (*Harery Kedem*, Part 2, p. 213)

This recounting of the redemption from Egypt goes on throughout all of Jewish history. Once God revealed Himself, as was needed in the time of Egypt, we must utilize this unique event to help with our own advancement in every generation. But I think that the visual and imaginative opportunities of the *seder* are particularly relevant to a sense-immersed society such as the present one we live in. Perhaps we are free of the idolatry of Egypt, but we are certainly living in a highly sensual Egypt-like society where pleasures, natural and unnatural, are rampant and continually placed before us by media in ways designed to be most enticing. We are, in many ways, similar to the Jewish people living in Egypt at the times of the Pharaoh. Most of us are also somewhat exhausted by the pace of modern Jewish life and the many family, financial and other stresses we experience, similar to the "shortness of breath" the Jews in Egypt experienced because of their intense labors. We too are in a compromised position when it comes to the ability to note and respond to the more subtle aspects of God's presence in the world.

The Role of the Observant Artist in Communicating Torah in Contemporary Times

The artist is the master of communicating ideas and feelings through the path of the senses. Whether it be a visual-based art form utilizing images, an auditory-based art form using music and poetry, or a combination of these, the artist has an important role in expressing through the senses, the ideas, concepts, emotions and experience of a life imbued with Torah and the worship of God. The qualitative, direct sense experience of the world is rich with meaning, whether natural or contrived by the artist. Within this arena the artist can shape and form the sense experience to create a powerful, positive impact. I will conclude this analysis with a statement from Rabbi Soloveitchik's essay "Lonely Man of Faith" and his description of the aspect of man's soul that senses the divine within the direct qualitative experience of the world.

> ..he (the man of faith known as Adam the second-RB) wants to understand the living, "given" world into which he has been cast. Therefore, he does not mathematize phenomena or conceptualize things. He encounters the universe in all its colorfulness, splendor, and grandeur,

and studies with the *naivete*, awe, and admiration of the child who seeks the unusual and wonderful in very ordinary thing and event. … Adam the second is receptive and beholds the world in its original dimensions. He looks for the Image of God not in the mathematical formula of the natural relational law but in every beam of light, in every bud and blossom, in the morning breeze and the stillness of a starlit evening." (Lonely Man of Faith p. 23)

POETRY ON THE PARSHA

Rabbi Meir used to say: "the dust of the first man was gathered from the whole world." (Sanhedrin 20). "And He fashioned…man dust"- Rabbi Yehuda. Rabbi Bar Simon said: "A young deer" (Beresheit Rabba-14). Note:(- the poem playing on the similarity in Hebrew, between the word for "dust" (*ahphar*) and that for "young deer" (*ohpher*)- a similarity evident in the quotation. The title of the poem, an unvowelized *ayin-pai-raysh,* can mean either one.

A Young Deer/Dust by Hemda Roth (a poet living in Jerusalem)

I was never there. But I know the cave and the many slippery paths to the pond.
(The mincing walk of the does around it left hearts in the fine sand.)
A sloping wall, bubbling, and the beating of drops.
A crack in the rock and light on its way to water.
Two wild goats bent over to drink, and a ruddy goat raised his head.
The shadow of his antlers in the pond-windows with panes of softness.
(His kisses-a trace of colors on the pond's skin, like sand.)

The Song by Hemda Roth

The song! The song!
In the dark stream the fish weave it around their bodies and unravel upon the water.
A silver fish sails, pulling the threads, hanging clouds on the wind.
Waves rise to become fins of cloud and fall to crawl upon the sand.
One more melody is buried dumb among the corals.
Look, the little fish burst forth rising like bubbles of song.
It comes back into my body night after night unraveling in me like dark water.

An Untitled Poem by Emily Dickenson (all her poems were untitled)

Bloom upon the Mountain, stated,
Blameless of a name.
Efflorescence of a Sunset-
Reproduced, the same.

Seed, had I, my purple sowing
Should endow the Day,
Not a tropic of the twilight
Show itself away.
Who for tilling, to the Mountain
Come, and disappear-
Whose be Her renown, or fading,
Witness, is not here.

While I state-the solemn petals
Far as North and East,
Far as South and West expanding,
Culminate in rest.

And the Mountain to the Evening
Fit His countenance,
Indicating by no muscles
The Experience.

Design by Robert Frost

I found a dimpled spider, fat and white,
On a white heal-all, holding up a moth
Like a white piece of rigid satin cloth --
Assorted characters of death and blight
Mixed ready to begin the morning right,
Like the ingredients of a witches' broth --
A snow-drop spider, a flower like a froth,
And dead wings carried like a paper kite.

What had that flower to do with being white,
The wayside blue and innocent heal-all?
What brought the kindred spider to that height,
Then steered the white moth thither in the night?
What but design of darkness to appall?--
If design govern in a thing so small.

PAINTINGS ON THE PARSHA

Creativity and the Senses

Curiously, God manifests Himself to both the Jewish people and the Egyptian people in a series of intensely physical experiences. The plagues that finally convince Egypt to free their Jewish slaves are uniquely physical spectacles guaranteed to impress. There seems to be not a trace of spirituality in the entire episode. As Nahshon ben Amminadav walks bravely into the sea, he is almost totally immersed before the sea will split for him and the rest of the people to enter.

Nahshon ben Amminadav Enters the Sea by Richard McBee

Similarly, the Exodus itself shows the entire Jewish people embraced by the parted waters that tower over them. The core experience is to become physically engulfed by God's power and might.

Exodus by Richard McBee

BO
CREATIVITY & COMPENSATION

In the *parsha* of Bo we find that God tells Moshe to be sure to remind the people to borrow (or request as gifts) valuables from their Egyptians neighbors–which we find here are surprisingly called "friends" *("ray-ay-hu")*.

Some commentators hold that the request was not to borrow these gold and silver vessels, but instead to request these items to possess permanently. God tells this to Moshe during the plague of darkness, but before the final plague of the death of the first born males. (Shemot 11:2)

2. Please, speak into the ears of the people, and let them borrow, each man from his <u>friend</u> and each woman from her friend, silver vessels and golden vessels."	ב. דַּבֶּר נָא בְּאָזְנֵי הָעָם וְיִשְׁאֲלוּ אִישׁ ׀ מֵאֵת <u>רֵעֵהוּ</u> וְאִשָּׁה מֵאֵת רְעוּתָהּ כְּלֵי כֶסֶף וּכְלֵי זָהָב:
Rashi: Please, speak- Heb. נָא-דַבֶּר is only an expression of request. [The verse is saying] I ask you to warn them about this, [i.e., to ask their neighbors for vessels] so that the righteous man, Abraham, will not say He fulfilled with them [His promise] "and they will enslave them and oppress them" (Gen. 15:13), but He did not fulfill with them "afterwards they will go forth with great possessions" (Gen. 15:14). — [from Ber. 9a]	דבר נא: אין נא אלא לשון בקשה, בבקשה ממך הזהירם על כך שלא יאמר אותו צדיק אברהם (בראשית טו יג) ועבדום וענו אותם קיים בהם, (שם יד) ואחרי כן יצאו ברכוש גדול לא קיים בהם:

3. So the Lord gave the people favor in Pharaoh's eyes; also the man Moses was highly esteemed in the eyes of Pharaoh's servants and in the eyes of the people.	ג. וַיִּתֵּן יְהוָה אֶת חֵן הָעָם בְּעֵינֵי מִצְרָיִם גַּם הָאִישׁ מֹשֶׁה גָּדוֹל מְאֹד בְּאֶרֶץ מִצְרַיִם בְּעֵינֵי עַבְדֵי פַרְעֹה וּבְעֵינֵי הָעָם:

There are a number of striking features to this request. First, why is the term *"ray-ay-hu"* used by God to describe the Egyptians relationship to the Jews? Weren't the Egyptians the persecutors and oppressors of the Jews? Weren't the Jews viewed by them as traitorous and dangerous aliens? Also, why did God use the opening word *"na"* ("if you please") in his statement to Moshe, which Rashi explains as God making a request of Moshe and not giving him a command. Rashi seems to imply that Moshe is, so to speak, "doing God a favor" so that Abraham won't be able to "call God to task" for only fulfilling the oppression of the Jews which was promised in the vision of the *Bris Ben HaBasarim*, but not fulfilling the promise to Abraham in that vision, that the Jews would "go forth with great possessions"! Why is God concerned with what Abraham will think! Why doesn't God then simply give a command that to Moshe and dispel with the *"na"* form of request? Also later, in Chapter 12, immediately <u>after</u> the plague of the death of the first born, the Torah states:

35. And the children of Israel did according to Moses' order, and they borrowed from the Egyptians silver objects, golden objects, and garments.	לה. וּבְנֵי יִשְׂרָאֵל עָשׂוּ כִּדְבַר מֹשֶׁה וַיִּשְׁאֲלוּ מִמִּצְרַיִם כְּלֵי כֶסֶף וּכְלֵי זָהָב וּשְׂמָלֹת:
Rashi: according to Moses' order: that he said to them in Egypt: "and let them borrow, each man from his friend" (Exod. 11:2). [from Mechilta]	כדבר משה: שאמר להם במצרים (לעיל יא ב) וישאלו איש מאת רעהו:

ושמלת: אף הן היו חשובות להם מן הכסף ומן הזהב, והמאוחר בפסוק חשוב:	and garments: These meant more to them than the silver and the gold, and [thus] whatever is mentioned later in the verse is more esteemed. — [from Mechilta]
לו. וַיהוָה נָתַן אֶת חֵן הָעָם בְּעֵינֵי מִצְרַיִם וַיַּשְׁאִלוּם וַיְנַצְּלוּ אֶת מִצְרָיִם:	36. The Lord gave the people favor in the eyes of the Egyptians, and they lent them, and they emptied out Egypt.
וישאלום: אף מה שלא היו שואלים מהם היו נותנים להם. אתה אומר אחד, טול שנים ולך:	and they lent them: Even what they [the Israelites] did not request, they [the Egyptians] gave them. You say, "[Lend me] one." [They responded,] "Take two and go!" -[from Mechilta]
וינצלו: ורוקינו:	and they emptied out: Heb. וַיְנַצְּלוּ. Onkelos renders: וְרוֹקִינוּ, and they emptied out.

The verses here are also very difficult to understand. How was it accomplished that "the Lord gave the people favor in the eyes of the Egyptians"? It seems that the Egyptians would have given the Jews whatever they wanted out of sheer terror, just to get them to leave following the final plague, even if God had not given the Jews favor in the eyes of the Egyptians! Also, we can ask, how was this "favor" was brought about? Did God "soften" the Egyptians hearts, similar to his method of hardening he heart of Pharaoh? And why was this necessary? Did the Jews care so much about the favor of the Egyptians? It seems that they did and this is shown by an interesting detail. We see that Rashi explains from the Mechilta that the people valued the clothes more than the silver and gold, ("is more esteemed")-presumably because it was a more personal object that the more valuable gold and silver vessels were. Finally, is what went on here really a "request", since the Egyptians were terrified of dying after the widespread death of the first born in every household?

Going back to the vision of Abraham at the *Bris Ben Ha-Basarim*, and looking at it in light of the Rashi regarding "*na*" and Abraham, it seems that the two aspects of the Jews time in Egypt that were revealed to Abraham –1) the oppression of the Jewish people and 2) their leaving with great wealth, are conceived as a paired unit, as if the oppression would not have been effective without the other part- the leaving with great wealth. How are these two aspects of the Jews experience in Egypt related?

One prominent view of this event is that the gold and silver vessels were a form of payment owed to the Jewish people for the years of unpaid labor. In the Talmud (Sanhedrin) there is a discussion of an incident in which the Egyptians went to Alexander the Great whose empire included both Egypt and Israel. They complained about the Jews taking these valuables from the Egyptians, as described in this current Torah portion. The Egyptians asked Alexander to force the Jews to "Return us the silver and gold that you took from us". Saviha ben Pasisa replied to them, "Return to me the wages of the six hundred thousand you enslaved in Egypt." (Sanhedrin 91A)

A commentary by an early 20th century scholar, Benno Jacob, explains that this occurrence lessened the bitterness the Jews felt towards to Egyptians, as we are commanded "you shall not abhor the Egyptian, for you were a stranger in his land". According to Jacob, the Jews also took instruction from this act regarding how to treat a slave when one releases him or her, in that one should send them away with the wealth they require to live independently. He states:

> ...the Torah records that the Egyptians and Jews parted as friends, the former, liberally furnishing them with gifts as the latter themselves had been bidden, in the case of send away their own Hebrew servants. Consequently "thou shalt not abhor an Egyptian, for thou wert a stranger in his land." But since the Egyptians could not be expected to offer gifts of their own initiative, Israel was bidden to spur them to do it and say to them": Let us part friends and we'll take with us a parting gift. ("God and Pharaoh", 1924)

These explanations though, do not explain the enigmatic Rashi, based on the Mechilta, which we described as having God "request" ("*na*") of Moshe to please remind the Jews to take or borrow the Egyptian's valuables for concern by God that Abraham will say that God only fulfilled the oppression portion of the vision in the *Bris Ben HaBasarim* and not the portion regarding "leaving with great wealth." Perhaps we can approach this difficult Mechilta by understanding the concept of a *bris* or covenant. In essence a covenant is an agreement that two parties enter into voluntarily and who are then bound by its terms. Rabbi Soloveitchik ("the Rav") in his essay "Lonely Man of Faith", explains that that the Jewish covenant is between two parties – God and the Jewish people, and that both entered into it voluntarily and both are, therefore, bound by its terms. Of course, God is the Creator and *Melech* (King) of the universe and rules with absolute authority. However, the Rav makes it abundantly clear in this essay, that despite this, God is equally bound by a covenant that he enters in to. The Rav explains:

> The element of togetherness of God and man is indispensable for the covenantal community, for the very validity of the covenant rests upon the juridic-Halakhic principle of free negotiation, mutual assumption of duties, and full recognition of the equal rights of both parties concerned with the covenant. Bother parties entering a

> covenantal relationship possess inalienable rights which may only be surrendered by mutual consent. The paradoxical experience of freedom, reciprocity, and "equality" in one's personal confrontation with God is basic for the understanding of the covenantal faith community. (Lonely Man of Faith, 44-45)

This striking idea, that God is "bound" by the covenant he has made with the Jewish people can be utilized to explain the *Mechilta's* commentary quoted by Rashi, regarding the term "*na*" – "please" that precedes God's statement to Moshe to remind the Jews to borrow or take possession of the valuables. Since God had entered into a covenantal arrangement with Abraham at the *Bris ben Ha-basarim* (the "Covenant Between the Parts") God too was bound by its stipulations. At the core of this agreement was that the Jews would be oppressed in a strange land and leave with great wealth. If the leaving with great wealth is not accomplished, then the oppression is not valid or "legal", so to speak. God is required to "fulfill His part of the bargain", which is that the Jews will leave with great wealth. He must deliver on this agreement and so the language of "*na*" reflects the position that God "needs" the Jews to cooperate so that the covenant can be fulfilled and God can be within his right, according to the covenant, to have enslaved the Jews. As they say, "a deal is a deal". This concept of the covenant is not contradicted by God being the absolute ruler of the universe. If God enters an agreement, the agreement is binding upon Him. That is God's will. If His will is to carry something out without an agreement he can justly do this as well, since all the universe is completely His to do with as he pleases. In the case of the *Bris ben Habasarim*, it was His will to enter into a covenant with the Jewish people.

The Wealth of Egypt as Compensation for the Oppression and Enslavement

Let us take a bold step and ask the following question: Why did the Jewish people have to be oppressed and enslaved in Egypt for so many years? What was the sin or sins for which they were being punished? Unlike the Jewish exiles which our tradition attributes to specific sins, we are not informed of any particular sin that was responsible for this enduring torment. In the *Hagaddah*, which recounts the enslavement and Exodus we do not find any mention of a sin for which the Jews are oppressed and enslaved. It is true that the enslavement is attributed to an enduring characteristic of humanity that "in every generation" there are those that seek our destruction. The *Haggadah* focuses on the praising of God for our redemption from servitude. But why were the Jewish people enslaved there in the first place? Is it conceivable that there <u>was</u> no sin or flaw that the Jewish people had that required our enslavement and torment in Egypt? If so, then why were the Jewish people placed there? I would like to suggest that we were placed there because it was necessary for the Jewish people's development as a holy nation. The Jewish people needed to be born as a nation in servitude to have servitude within its "national DNA". Only through this process could the Jewish nation become the enduring servants of God that is at the core Jewish mission. The Jewish people also needed to learn compassion for, and valuing of, the disenfranchised, the stranger, the defenseless, in order to be the people who model justice and mercy for the world. The enslavement in Egypt was necessary for the "engineering "of the Jewish people to function as a "light to the nations of the world."

This perspective of the purpose for being subjected to the tortures of Egypt may also shed some light on the concept of

God's stating "*na*" –"please" to Moses, regarding the Jews requesting of the valuables from the Egyptians and the "emptying out" of the nation. Although, as we said, God is the absolute ruler of the world and can subject man to whatever is His will. But God acts towards the Jewish people in a manner by which they can learn justice and mercy and "walk in His ways". With this in mind, God, entered the covenant with them and, so to speak, "owes" the Jewish people compensation for their enduring of the slavery, which was required of them in order to become the holy nation which God's willed them to be- to be the people who would be "*m-takkin*" the world (repair it) and remove the idolatry that separated humanity from its perception of and connection to the Creator. In this way, the gold and silver were a form of restitution for the Jewish people for what they had to endure to fulfill their holy mission.

Perhaps a *mushal* (story) will be helpful here. What if we needed to send our children into a painful, torturous situation, not due to any fault of their own, but to prepare them for a great mission. Once they had gone through the torment of the preparation, it would be incumbent upon us, out of justice, mercy and love, to comfort, strengthen and appease them to the greatest extent, not only to heal the wounds that this preparation required of them, but also in restitution for what we had put them through. From this approach the gold and silver vessels were restitution for the torment that God put the Jewish people through to prepare them for their role in human history.

A quote from Rabbi Solovetichik's lecture "The Duty of the King" expresses the idea that the glory of God is accomplished through the role of the Jewish people in history. He states:

The Midrash says several times that the defeat of the Jewish people is as if the *Ribono-shel-Olam* (God: Master of the World) has been defeated. A victory on the part of the Jewish people is also a triumph for the Ribono-shel-Olam...The State of Israel is truly a victory for the *Ribono-shel-Olam*. It is a *Kiddush Hashem*, a sanctification of the Almighty's Name! "And I will be sanctified in you in the sight of the nations" (Ezekiel 20:41). A political defeat of the Jewish people actually impairs, so to speak, the Kingdom of the Almighty. People then say of our Bible, prophets, and patriarchs that they are a hoax....When the Jew fights a war, it is not only for himself but for the Name of the Almighty....I have no doubt that the War of Independence (1948-RB) and the Six-Day War (1967-RB) were wars fought for the Almighty. These wars changed the climate and enhanced the prestige of the Jew. In Judaism, the prestige of the Jew is identical with the majesty of God. This is exactly what Maimonides meant when he said that the king "must fight the wars of the Almighty" (Mishneh Torah, Hilkhot Melakhim 4:10). (From the book "The Rav: The World of Rabbi Joseph B. Soloveitchik – Volume 2:127-130)

The Jewish Scholar, the Jewish Artist and the Role of Compensation

We observe from this incident of the Jewish people's request for gold and silver vessels that compensation is an essential requirement in the just treatment of a person. Although the concept of fair compensation may seem obvious to us, it is less universal when we speak of the religious experience. Religion often glorifies the sacrifice of one's material possession and the embracing of poverty as ideals that reflect one's disinterest in the mundane things of this world. Christianity and Hinduism are prominent examples of religions that idealize poverty and the "holy man" who withdraws from the things of the material world to "dwell with God" in a monastery or on a remote mountaintop.

In the Jewish tradition we know that the patriarchs Abraham, Isaac and Jacob were people of great wealth. We see on many instances the wealth is not, it seems, contrary to wisdom and even, prophecy. What is extremely important is the just and fair utilization of the wealth and that meticulous attention is paid to justice and honesty with regards to monetary manners. Perhaps one of the most intriguing statements regarding this connection of a wise person to their wealth is cited by Rashi with regards to Jacob's returning to the camp on the evening before the momentous occasion of meeting his very dangerous brother Esau. This is the evening he wrestled with a mysterious man (or according to Maimonides, had a prophetic vision of wrestling with a mysterious man), considered by most commentators to be the guardian angel of Esau. Why did Jacob return to the camp after he had removed his family to two other camps that were more protected from a possible attack from his brother? Rashi states:

25. And Jacob was left alone, and a man wrestled with him until the break of dawn.	כה. וַיִּוָּתֵר יַעֲקֹב לְבַדּוֹ וַיֵּאָבֵק אִישׁ עִמּוֹ עַד עֲלוֹת הַשָּׁחַר:
And Jacob was left: He had forgotten small bottles and returned for them. — [from Gen. Rabbah 77:2, Chullin 91a]	ויותר יעקב: שכח פכים קטנים וחזר עליהם:

From this episode, our Rabbis have made the cryptic statement that "a Torah scholar's possessions are more precious to him, than his body." Why? Perhaps because the possessions are the result of just acquisition and he has a clear and absolute right to them. His body is a gift of God, acquired with no transaction or toil. I don't think the statement means to convey that there is an intense level of attachment that a scholar has to his or her possessions. Instead, it is brought to clarify that one's possessions are not to be viewed at all negatively, if acquired honestly, and that justice is equally important when one considers what one has a right to possess, as much as when one considers what one does not have a right to possess. One must view oneself as someone who has to be treated with the same meticulous level of fairness that a truly just person would treat friends and neighbors or anyone that he or she has business or monetary dealing with. Put succinctly, one is required to be just and fair to oneself in monetary matters, just like one would be to anyone else. Perhaps this concept, which is fundamental to the Jewish worldview, is why Jews have a reputation among many, of being overly focused on commerce. This focus, I believe, is looked at with some disdain by other religions as being a flaw and a focus on the mundane and acquisitive instinct. But in its best form, this focus of Jewish law and scholarship on monetary matters reflects an interest in the making of this world a just and holy one, here and now, as opposed to casting our view and attention to the next world or to the time after the coming of the Messiah. The "this worldly" aspect of Judaism has been discussed often by Rabbi Joseph B. Soloveitchik, in his text "Halakhic Man". He states there:

> Halakhic man (basically, an observant Jew who draws from Jewish law, the structure and meaning of his life-RB), however, takes up his position in this world and does not move from it. He wishes to purify this world, not to escape from it. "Flight goeth before a fall. (*Sotah* 8:6)" Halakhic man is characterized by a powerful stiff-neckedness and stubbornness. He fights against life's evil and struggles relentlessly with the wicked kingdom and with all the hosts of iniquity in the cosmos. His goal is not flight to another world that is wholly good, but rather bringing down that eternal world into the midst of our world. *Homo religiosus* (very basically, a religious person whose focus is a direct connection to God through breaking out of the mundane bounds of this world-RB), his glance fixed upon higher realms, forgets all too

> frequently the lower realms and becomes ensnared in the sins of ethical inconsistency and hypocrisy. See what many religions have done to this world on account of their yearning to break through the bounds of concrete reality and escape to the sphere of eternity. They have been so intoxicated by their dreams of an exalted supernal existence that they have failed to hear the cries of "them that dwell in houses of clay" (Job 4:19), the sighs of the orphans, the groans of the destitute. Had they not desired to unite with infinity and to merge with transcendence, then they might have been able to do something to aid the widow and orphan, to save the oppressed from the hand of the oppressor. There is nothing so physically and spiritually destructive as diverting one's attention from this world. (Halakhic Man, p. 41)

The Jewish scholar or artist, it follows, should be passionate and dedicated to receiving fair payment and compensation for himself, as much as he should be with anyone else. It is true that with regards to the Jewish scholar being paid for teaching Torah there are certain restrictions and much discussion. With regards to the oral law (teaching of Talmud and the Jewish legal system), Maimonides held that payment was not permitted. Since the oral law has been passed down from God to Moshe at "no charge" and from him to the maintainers of our tradition (*baaley mesorah*) for no charge, one should not charge for the continuance of this process. However, there are many issues regarding this prohibition. According to some, payment is an absolute necessity today in order to prevent the complete loss of Torah scholarship and Torah law. Also, there are formulations of this payment to teachers of Torah, not for the teaching of the oral Torah per se, but for the time one would have spent otherwise in a different occupation. Alternatively, some hold that the payment is for classroom management and related activities connected to the teacher's job.

Regarding the Jewish artist, there is no similar restriction. However, the Jewish artist, similar to artists in general, does not necessarily see him or herself as performing "work for hire" per se. The creation of art is a result of not only technical talent, but an inspiration and desire to express some type of truth or insight. There is the popular ideal of the "starving artist" who labors in total obscurity and poverty with a burning desire to bring forth his or her vision to the world, regardless of recognition or compensation. Vincent Van Gogh and Paul Gauguin are perhaps the most famous examples of this ideal. Struggling in total poverty, obscurity and illness they brought forth paintings of great beauty, which communicated unique dimensions of existence, previously undepicted.

I don't know if Jewish artists, or very many artists of any type today, feel any ambiguity regarding compensation for their art. The world is so hyper-focused on financial success, that I am sure it has also penetrated the artistic community. We, of course, read in the New York Times about the astronomical prices paid by billionaires to possess prized painting and sculptures. But still, I would think that the dedicated artist, like any other inspired creative person, views the bringing forth of their creations to be a good in itself, even if it is not recognized or compensated. From our discussion regarding the role of compensation in Judaism, I would just like to conclude with the thought that there should be no conflict regarding payment for art. Judaism, as we have tried to show, does not share the notion propounded by the other religions, that compensation somehow, necessarily besmirches or diminishes the religious or creative experience. On the contrary, we see, even the Creator of the Universe was careful to make sure that the Jewish people were compensated as part of the redemption process from Egypt.

POETRY ON THE PARSHA

Below are poems that are relevant to our discussion:

Provide, Provide   by Robert Frost

The witch that came (the withered hag) to wash the steps with pail and rag
Was once the beauty Abishag,
The picture pride of Hollywood.
Too many fall from great and good
For you to doubt the likelihood.
Die early and avoid the fate.
Or if predestined to die late, make up your mind to die in state.
Make the whole stock exchange your own! If need be occupy a throne,
Where nobody can call you crone.
Some have relied on what they knew, others on being simply true.
What worked for them might work for you.
No memory of having starred atones for later disregard
Or keeps the end from being hard.
Better to go down dignified with boughten friendship at your side
Than none at all. Provide, provide!

Richard Cory by Edwin Arlington Robinson

Whenever Richard Cory went down town,
We people on the pavement looked at him:
He was a gentleman from sole to crown,
Clean favored, and imperially slim.

And he was always quietly arrayed,
And he was always human when he talked;
But still he fluttered pulses when he said,
'Good-morning,' and he glittered when he walked.

And he was rich - yes, richer than a king -
And admirably schooled in every grace:
In fine, we thought that he was everything
To make us wish that we were in his place.

So on we worked, and waited for the light,
And went without the meat, and cursed the bread;
And Richard Cory, one calm summer night,
Went home and put a bullet through his head.

Money by C.K. Williams

How did money get into the soul; how did base dollars and cents ascend
From the slime
To burrow their way into the crannies of consciousness, even it feels like
Into the flesh?

Wants with no object, needs with no end, like bacteria bringing their
Fever and freezing,
Viruses gnawing at neurons, infecting even the sanctuaries of altruism
And self-worth

We asked soul to be huge, encompassing, sensitive, knowing, all-knowing,
But not this,
Not money roaring in with battalions of pluses and minus, setting up camps of profit and loss,

Not joy become calculation, life counting itself, compounding itself like
A pocket of pebbles:
Sorrow, it feels like; a weeping, unhealable wound, an affront at all costs
To be avenged

From the Second Chapter of Kohetes (Ecclesiastes)

4. I made myself great works; I built myself houses, and I planted myself vineyards	ד. הִגְדַּלְתִּי מַעֲשָׂי בָּנִיתִי לִי בָּתִּים נָטַעְתִּי לִי כְּרָמִים:
5. I made myself gardens and orchards, and I planted in them all sorts of fruit trees.	ה. עָשִׂיתִי לִי גַּנּוֹת וּפַרְדֵּסִים וְנָטַעְתִּי בָהֶם עֵץ כָּל פֶּרִי:
6. I made myself pools of water, to water from them a forest sprouting with trees.	ו. עָשִׂיתִי לִי בְּרֵכוֹת מָיִם לְהַשְׁקוֹת מֵהֶם יַעַר צוֹמֵחַ עֵצִים:
7. I acquired male and female slaves, and I had household members; also I had possession of cattle and flocks, more than all who were before me in Jerusalem.	ז. קָנִיתִי עֲבָדִים וּשְׁפָחוֹת וּבְנֵי בַיִת הָיָה לִי גַּם מִקְנֶה בָקָר וָצֹאן הַרְבֵּה הָיָה לִי מִכֹּל שֶׁהָיוּ לְפָנַי בִּירוּשָׁלָֹם:
8. I accumulated for myself also silver and gold, and the treasures of the kings and the provinces; I acquired for myself various types of musical instruments, the delight of the sons of men, wagons and coaches.	ח. כָּנַסְתִּי לִי גַּם כֶּסֶף וְזָהָב וּסְגֻלַּת מְלָכִים וְהַמְּדִינוֹת עָשִׂיתִי לִי שָׁרִים וְשָׁרוֹת וְתַעֲנֻגוֹת בְּנֵי הָאָדָם שִׁדָּה וְשִׁדּוֹת:
9. So I became great, and I increased more than all who were before me in Jerusalem; also my wisdom remained with me.	ט. וְגָדַלְתִּי וְהוֹסַפְתִּי מִכֹּל שֶׁהָיָה לְפָנַי בִּירוּשָׁלָֹם אַף חָכְמָתִי עָמְדָה לִּי:

10. And [of] all that my eyes desired I did not deprive them; I did not deprive my heart of any joy, but my heart rejoiced with all my toil, and this was my portion from all my toil.	י. וְכֹל אֲשֶׁר שָׁאֲלוּ עֵינַי לֹא אָצַלְתִּי מֵהֶם לֹא מָנַעְתִּי אֶת לִבִּי מִכָּל שִׂמְחָה כִּי לִבִּי שָׂמֵחַ מִכָּל עֲמָלִי וְזֶה הָיָה חֶלְקִי מִכָּל עֲמָלִי:
<u>11</u>. Then I turned [to look] at all my deeds that my hands had wrought and upon the toil that I had toiled to do, and behold everything is vanity and frustration, and there is no profit under the	יא. וּפָנִיתִי אֲנִי בְּכָל מַעֲשַׂי שֶׁעָשׂוּ יָדַי וּבֶעָמָל שֶׁעָמַלְתִּי לַעֲשׂוֹת וְהִנֵּה הַכֹּל הֶבֶל וּרְעוּת רוּחַ וְאֵין יִתְרוֹן תַּחַת הַשָּׁמֶשׁ:

PAINTINGS ON THE PARSHA

Below are images from art selected by the artist Richard McBee, with Mr. McBee's commentary. This images are relevant to the subject matter of this analysis. Mr. McBee's art and writings can be found at http://richardmcbee.com/

Creativity and Compensation
Terror is an emotion that drives much of the Torah narrative in the Exodus tales. Its foundation is in the Book of Genesis beginning with the Covenant Between the Parts. As a forbidding darkness descends upon Abraham, birds of prey swoop down on the sacrifices Abraham has prepared. He is then given the fearful prophecy that foretells the enslavement of the Jewish people. But there is hope because they will ultimately redeemed and given great wealth.

Covenant Between the Parts by Richard McBee

Similarly the birth of Moses is overshadowed by the Egyptian terror of the slaughter of all male Jewish infants. His bravely heroic sister, Miriam, narrowly saves Moses as she flees the family house. (R.M.)

Miriam Saves the Infant Moses by Richard McBee

Finally, the Plague of the Firstborn is the terrifying catastrophe that actually inaugurates the freedom of the Jewish people. The cost in human lives, innocent and guilty, is awesome. (R.M.)

The Plague of the First Born by Richard McBee

BESHALLACH
CREATIVITY, CATHARSIS & THE SONG BY THE SEA

In the parsha of Beshallach the Jewish people are saved from Pharaoh's charioteers in a most dramatic and miraculous fashion. The Sea of Reeds splits forming walls of water on each side and the Jewish people pass through while the Egyptians are prevented from following after them by a pillar of fire. Once the Jewish people have passed through the sea to the other side, the pillar of fire is removed and the Egyptians drive on into the sea which is still miraculously cleaved in two. Once the Egyptian forces enter the dry seabed, God returns the waters to their place, drowning the Egyptian forces. The Torah states:

26. Thereupon, the Lord said to Moses, Stretch out your hand over the sea, and let the water return upon the Egyptians, upon their chariots, and upon their horsemen.	כו. וַיֹּאמֶר יְהֹוָה אֶל מֹשֶׁה נְטֵה אֶת יָדְךָ עַל הַיָּם וְיָשֻׁבוּ הַמַּיִם עַל מִצְרַיִם עַל רִכְבּוֹ וְעַל פָּרָשָׁיו:
27. So Moses stretched out his hand over the sea, and toward morning the sea returned to its strength, as the Egyptians were fleeing toward it, and the Lord stirred the Egyptians into the sea.	כז. וַיֵּט מֹשֶׁה אֶת יָדוֹ עַל הַיָּם וַיָּשָׁב הַיָּם לִפְנוֹת בֹּקֶר לְאֵיתָנוֹ וּמִצְרַיִם נָסִים לִקְרָאתוֹ וַיְנַעֵר יְהֹוָה אֶת מִצְרַיִם בְּתוֹךְ הַיָּם:
28. And the waters returned and covered the chariots and the horsemen, the entire force of Pharaoh coming after them into the sea; not even one of them survived.	כח. וַיָּשֻׁבוּ הַמַּיִם וַיְכַסּוּ אֶת הָרֶכֶב וְאֵת הַפָּרָשִׁים לְכֹל חֵיל פַּרְעֹה הַבָּאִים אַחֲרֵיהֶם בַּיָּם לֹא נִשְׁאַר בָּהֶם עַד אֶחָד:
29. But the children of Israel went on dry land in the midst	כט. וּבְנֵי יִשְׂרָאֵל הָלְכוּ בַיַּבָּשָׁה

of the sea, and the water was to them like a wall from their right and from their left.	בְּתוֹךְ הַיָּם וְהַמַּיִם לָהֶם חֹמָה מִימִינָם וּמִשְּׂמֹאלָם:
30. On that day the Lord saved Israel from the hand[s] of the Egyptians, and Israel saw the Egyptians dying on the seashore.	ל. וַיּוֹשַׁע יְהֹוָה בַּיּוֹם הַהוּא אֶת יִשְׂרָאֵל מִיַּד מִצְרָיִם וַיַּרְא יִשְׂרָאֵל אֶת מִצְרַיִם מֵת עַל שְׂפַת הַיָּם:
31. And Israel saw the great hand, which the Lord had used upon the Egyptians, and the people feared the Lord, and they believed in the Lord and in Moses, His servant.	לא. וַיַּרְא יִשְׂרָאֵל אֶת הַיָּד הַגְּדֹלָה אֲשֶׁר עָשָׂה יְהֹוָה בְּמִצְרַיִם וַיִּירְאוּ הָעָם אֶת יְהֹוָה וַיַּאֲמִינוּ בַּיהֹוָה וּבְמֹשֶׁה עַבְדּוֹ:

(Shemot 14: 26-31)

This final destruction of the Egyptian army was the culmination of a process of redemption that began with the first of the plagues. It is this completion of the redemptive process and the death of the persecutors taking place here, which makes this event different in character from all of the great miracles that transpired throughout the previous year. It is at this point, with the dead Egyptian charioteers washed up on the beach at the foot of the Jewish people, that Moshe is inspired to compose the "Song by the Sea". He and Miriam sing this song with the Jewish people.

1. Then Moses and the children of Israel sang this song to the Lord, and they spoke, saying, I will sing to the Lord, for very exalted is He; a horse and its rider He cast into the sea. (Shemot 15:1)	א. אָז יָשִׁיר מֹשֶׁה וּבְנֵי יִשְׂרָאֵל אֶת הַשִּׁירָה הַזֹּאת לַיהֹוָה וַיֹּאמְרוּ לֵאמֹר אָשִׁירָה לַיהֹוָה כִּי גָאֹה גָּאָה סוּס וְרֹכְבוֹ רָמָה בַיָּם:

The song then continues for another 18 verses. The *Mechilta* (15.1) holds that there are ten divinely inspired songs within the Jewish tradition. Nine of these songs have already been composed, with the tenth to be composed by the Messiah. Below is a list of the 10 songs, with brief descriptions.

TORAH TOP 10 (ONLY 10) SONGS OF ALL TIME!

Song Name	Composer(s)	Singer	Content/Background
Song of Adam (A Psalm for the Sabbath Day Ps. 92.1)	Adam Ha-Rishon	Adam Ha-Rishon	God's forgiveness and reduced punishment of Cain after Cain (Kayan) killed Abel (Hevel)
Song at the Sea	Moshe Rebbenu & Miriam	Moshe, Miriam and Jewish people	Praise of God's destroying of the Egyptians
Song of the Well	The Jewish People	The Jewish People	Praise for receiving water in the desert
HaAzinu	Moshe Rebbenu	Moshe Rebbenu	Review of his life, prophecies for future, composed shortly before his death
Song of Joshua	Joshua ben Nun	Joshua ben Nun	Sung by Joshua after he was able to the miraculous and climatic event when he stopped the sun and the moon by singing this song
Song of Devorah and Barak	Devorah and Barak	Devorah and Barak	Sung is praise of God for delivering Sisera, the Canaanite general into their hands. (The only duet of the ten songs)
Song of Hannah	Hannah	Hannah	Sung upon her conceiving and giving birth to a son (the prophet Samuel), after years of barrenness

Song of David	King David	King David	In praise of God for the miracles through which David was delivered from his enemies
Song of Songs	King Solomon	Unknown	Great love ballad between God and the Jewish people, highly allegorical
The Song of the World to Come	The Messiah	The Messiah (?)	Revealing the purpose and meaning of human history

We will try to understand what is the nature of a "song" that makes it different from prophecies, psalms or the other inspired compositions of our prophets and great scholars. I do not think that the uniqueness of a song lies in its being comprised of words set to music, as opposed to a poem, in which there isn't any music per se. As a matter of fact, our tradition holds that many of the psalms were sung by the Levites and pilgrims coming to Jerusalem during the festivals. So what then is it about the praise of God in these songs that is different than other forms of praise? In the Stone Chumash of the Art Scroll Series the commentary states regarding the Song by the Sea:

> In the Torah's definition, a "song" is a profound and unusual spiritual phenomenon; according to Mechilta 15:1, there were only ten songs from the beginning of Creation to the end of the Scriptural period. Even the sublime "poetry" of David and Isaiah, as well as that of the other prophets, is not among the ten songs. What then constitutes the Torah's concept of song? In the normal course of events, we fail to perceive the hand of God at work, and we often wonder how most of the daily seemingly unrelated phenomena surrounding us could be part of a Divine, coherent plan. We see suffering and evil and we wonder how they can be the handiwork of a Merciful God. Rarely, however-very rarely- there is a flash

> of insight that makes people realize how all the pieces of the puzzle fall into place. At such times, we can understand how every note, instrument, and participant in God's symphony of Creation plans its roles. The result is song, for the Torah's concept of song is the condition in which all the apparently unrelated and contradictory phenomena do indeed meld into a coherent, merciful, comprehensible whole.
>
> At the sea, Moses and the Jewish people understood their situation as never before. The suffering of the Egyptian exile, the deception that led Pharaoh to pursue them, the hopelessness they had felt when they were surrounded by Pharaoh, the sea, and the wilderness; the demands for many of their recrimination that his arrival in Egypt to carry out God's mission had only made things worse for Israel-such doubts and fears disappeared when the sea split and, as the Sages teach in Mechilta, even a simple maidservant at the sea perceived a higher degree of revelation than that of the prophet Ezekiel in his Heavenly vision, described in Ezekiel chapter 1. To the Jews at the sea, Creation became a symphony, a *song*, because they understood how every unrelated and incomprehensible event was part of the harmonious score that led up the greatest of all miracles. (p. 375)

In essence, this explanation holds that song is the result of a new level of clarification-"there is a flash of insight that makes people realize how all the pieces of the puzzle fall into place". This certainly does seem to fit the situation of the Song by the Sea, as the Jews had the opportunity to realize that the long drawn out and somewhat incomplete victory of the Egyptians up to this point, was "set up", so to speak, by God to be able to create this final, awe-inspiring conclusion. But, there is difficulty in applying this idea to the full list of 10 songs, listed above. Where did the clarity of seeing the harmony and meaning of events operate in the case the other songs? Perhaps in the case of Hannah one could say that she saw the meaning behind her suffering and barrenness in that it brought her to a level that was capable of bringing a great prophet such as Samuel to the world. But how do the other songs relate to this concept of "seeing the big picture"?

Songs and Catharsis

I would like to suggest an alternative factor as the common denominator in these ten songs. I believe that they can be seen to function as a particular type of catharsis for their composers and singers. Catharsis is a somewhat equivocal term, having a variety of meanings. Webster defines it as follows:

> The term "catharsis" (from the Greek (κάθαρσις) *katharsis* meaning "purification" or "cleansing") is the purification and purgation of emotions—especially pity and fear—through art- or any extreme change in emotion that results in renewal and restoration.

Aristotle's concept of catharsis in poetics and theater provides a mechanism that generates the rational control of irrational emotions. In a similar shade of meaning, in psychology, the term was first employed by Sigmund Freud's colleague Josef Breuer (1842–1925), who developed a well-known "cathartic" method of treatment using hypnosis for persons suffering from hysterical symptoms.

In the psychoanalytic method, patients were able to recall traumatic experiences, and through the process of expressing the original emotions that had been repressed and forgotten, they were relieved of their symptoms. Catharsis was central to Freud's concept of psychoanalysis. All of these commonly held interpretations of catharsis, purgation, purification, and clarification are considered by most scholars to represent a healing process through which an individual is freed of the irrational control of an emotion that has impaired clear thinking and constructive action. Rabbi Soloveitchik in his essay "Catharsis" describes this as being a process by which Jewish law redeems the person's emotion and intellectual life in a manner which he labels as cathartic. He explains that in times of victory and personal power, a person must often withdraw and stop, in obedience to God.

> The Halakchic catharsis expresses itself in paradoxical movement in two opposite directions – in surging forward boldly and in retreating humbly. Man's heroic experience is a polar, antithetic one. Man drives forward only to retreat and reverse, subsequently, the direction of his movement….Halacha teaches that at every level of our total existential experience- the aesthetic-hedonic, the emotional, the intellectual, the moral-religious-one must engage in the dialectical movement by alternately advancing and retreating. (Catharsis –Part 1-Section 6)

Particularly relevant to our discussion is the Rav's statements regarding the Jewish perspective on catharsis within the religious sphere. He states:

> There is an unredeemed moral and religious experience, as there is an unredeemed body and an unredeemed logos. Let us be candid: if one has not redeemed his religious life he may become self-righteous, insensitive, or even destructive. The story of the Crusades, the Inquisition, and other outbursts of religious fanaticism bear out this thesis. Judaism has sanctioned man, has stated that there is a spark of divinity in man; Judaism has never subscribed to the philosophy that man is intrinsically sinful. On the contrary, we have taught that the moral challenge which confronts man and the opportunities offered him are unlimited. Man, as seen by Judaism, is potentially a good, progressive being. However, man often finds himself in the grip on an overwhelming, irresistible force that pulls him downward. The ascent up the mount of the Lord often turns into a rapid descent down the mount. The impetuous and passionate rush toward God may suddenly become a flight from God. (Part 2: Section 4)

Rabbi Soloveitchik's perspective on catharsis is that it is needed for a person to guard against being overwhelmed by the lure of his personal drive toward self-importance/greatness, whether in the religious, scientific, emotional or physical spheres of life. I would interpret the Song at the Sea and the other songs mentioned above, as providing a catharsis and functioning as a way of directing and sublimating the potentially destructive impact that these close encounters with God could have had on those involved. Instead of drawing one closer to God and improving one's clarity about oneself and the world, the result of these encounters can instead result in a person cultivating a heightened sense of being chosen, of being special. This can quickly morph into a destructive delusion of personal greatness and infallibility. In the case of the Song of the Sea, the Jews who had been so denigrated in servitude to the Egyptians had now been miraculously saved from their oppressors. This was a dangerous time in which the feeling of being chosen mixed, perhaps, with the emotions of murderous revenge and sadistic joy, as the Jewish people viewed their tormenter and pursuers, drowned and lying dead at their feet on the seashore. We will look into the verses of the song to clarify the emotional states which were purged and redeemed by the Song of the Sea.

2. The Eternal's strength and His vengeance were my salvation; this is my God, and I will make Him a habitation, the God of my father, and I will ascribe to Him exaltation.	ב. עָזִּי וְזִמְרָת יָהּ וַיְהִי לִי לִישׁוּעָה זֶה אֵלִי וְאַנְוֵהוּ אֱלֹהֵי אָבִי וַאֲרֹמְמֶנְהוּ:
3. The Lord is a Master of war; the Lord is His Name.	ג. יְהוָה אִישׁ מִלְחָמָה יְהוָה שְׁמוֹ:
4. Pharaoh's chariots and his army He cast into the sea, and the elite of his officers sank in the Red Sea.	ד. מַרְכְּבֹת פַּרְעֹה וְחֵילוֹ יָרָה בַיָּם וּמִבְחַר שָׁלִשָׁיו טֻבְּעוּ בְיַם סוּף:
5. The depths covered them; they descended into the depths like a	ה. תְּהֹמֹת יְכַסְיֻמוּ יָרְדוּ בִמְצוֹלֹת כְּמוֹ אָבֶן:

stone.

6. Your right hand, O Lord, is most powerful; Your right hand, O Lord, crushes the foe.	ו. יְמִינְךָ יְהֹוָה נֶאְדָּרִי בַּכֹּחַ יְמִינְךָ יְהֹוָה תִּרְעַץ אוֹיֵב:
7. And with Your great pride You tear down those who rise up against You; You send forth Your burning wrath; it devours them like straw.	ז. וּבְרֹב גְּאוֹנְךָ תַּהֲרֹס קָמֶיךָ תְּשַׁלַּח חֲרֹנְךָ יֹאכְלֵמוֹ כַּקַּשׁ:

It is not uncommon that a people who have been severely oppressed and tormented by another, upon viewing the dramatic destruction of their oppressors will express the most vicious, sadistic feelings toward their vanquished foes. History is replete with slave rebellions that have been particularly horrific in the bloody vengeance they reeked upon their former oppressors. For the Jew, the drowning of the Egyptians at the Sea of Reeds and the emotional force it brought forth, needed to be "managed" and utilized for a positive, developmental purpose. This was especially important at this point for the Jewish people as they were in the formative stage of their development. The Song by the Sea took these feelings of joy at the vanquishing of their enemy and objectified them to clarify their understanding of God and His rule over the Earth.

The first lines of the song (verse 2) describe the act of being an act of God's vengeance ("His vengeance"), meaning the Egyptians were destroyed for their sin against God in rejecting His commands, and not simply because they were the enemy of the Jewish people. Their destruction is not simply the outcome of a "feud" of warring parties where God is "on our side". This act is the fulfillment of divine justice. This first verse also clarifies the Jewish people's obligation and need to praise God for this act, as it says "I will make him a habitation, the God of my father, I will ascribe to Him exaltation." The 6th and 7th verse also objectify this event as being one of God's justice and not simply "payback" or "revenge" for the Jewish people. "Your right hand, O Lord, crushes the foe. And with great pride You tear down those who rise up against You." Instead of this event degrading the Jewish people by becoming an opportunity for the venting of their lust for revenge, it is redeemed by this song and instead releases the Jewish people from their hatred and insecurity without being a primitive, gross outpouring of vengeful rage.

It is beyond the scope of this essay to explore the other songs of the Torah, but I do believe after reviewing them that they can also be viewed in this way. I am posing the idea that there was a cathartic benefit in each of these songs, with their sublimating and constructive channeling of the emotional outpourings that accompanied the events that inspired each of these songs. My conjecture is that without the cathartic impact of the song, these events had the potential to cause destructive transformations. When God performs wondrous things to the benefit of a person or people, the pride and sense of one's greatness can be greatly stimulated. This can destroy the soul of someone as surely as any crushing defeat. Throughout the history of the Jewish people it has been victories and successes that have led us away from God, more than our struggles and defeats.

POETRY ON THE PARSHA

Below is the Song of Devorah and Barak, which is the haftorah for the *parsha* of Beshallach. In this song Devorah and Barak recount the military defeat and annihilation of Sisera and his Canaanite army that have tormented the Jewish people in the land of Israel.

Song of Deborah

>1. Now Deborah and Barak the son of Abinoam sang on that day, saying.
>2. "When breaches are made in Israel, when the people offer themselves willingly, bless the Lord.
>3. Hear, O kings, give ear, O princes; I, to the Lord I shall sing, I shall sing to the Lord, the God of Israel.
>4. Lord, when You went forth out of Seir, when You marched out of the field of Edom, the earth trembled, the heavens also dripped; also the clouds dripped water.
>5. The mountains melted at the presence of the Lord, this (was at) Sinai, because of the presence of the Lord, the God of Israel.
>6. In the days of Shamgar the son of Anath, in the days of Jael, caravans ceased, and travelers walked on crooked paths.
>7. The open cities ceased, in Israel they ceased, until I Deborah arose; I arose as a mother in Israel.
>8. When they chose new gods, then there was war in the cities; was there seen a shield or a spear (when the) forty thousand (went against) Israel?
>9. My heart is toward the lawgivers of Israel, that offered themselves willingly among the people, (saying,) 'Bless the Lord.'
>10. The riders of white donkeys, those that sit in judgment, and those that walk on the path, tell of it.
>11. Instead of the noise of adversaries, between the places of drawing water, there they will tell the righteous acts of the Lord, the righteous acts of restoring open cities in Israel. Then the people of the Lord went down to the cities.
>12. Praise! Praise! Deborah. Praise! Praise! Utter a song. Arise Barak, and capture your captives, son of Abinoam.
>13. Then ruled a remnant among the mighty of the nations;

the Lord dominated the strong for me.

14. Out of Ephraim, whose root was against Amalek; after you (will be) Benjamin with your abaters; out of Machir came down officers, and out of Zebulun they that handle the pen of the scribe.

15. And the princes of Issachar were with Deborah, as was Issachar with Barak; into the valley they rushed forth with their feet. (But) among the divisions of Reuben, (there were) great resolves of heart.

16. Why do you sit between the borders, to hear the bleatings of the flocks? At the divisions of Reuben, (there are) great searchings of heart.

17. Gilead abides beyond the Jordan; and Dan, why does he gather into the ships? Asher dwelt at the shore of the seas, and by his breaches he abides.

18. Zebulun is a people that jeopardized their lives to die, as did Naphtali, upon the high places of the field.

19. The kings came and fought; then fought the kings of Canaan in Taanach by the waters of Megiddo; they took no gain of money.

20. From heaven they fought; the stars from their courses fought against Sisera.

21. The brook Kishon swept them away, that ancient brook, the brook Kishon; tread down, O my soul, (their) strength.

22. Then were pounded the heels of the horses by reason of the prancings, the prancings of their mighty ones.

23. 'Curse you Meroz,' said the messenger of the Lord, 'curse you bitterly (you) inhabitants thereof,' because they came not to the aid of the Lord, to the aid of the Lord against the mighty.

24. Blessed above women shall Jael, the wife of Heber the Kenite, be; above women in the tent shall she be blessed.

25. Water he requested, (but) milk she gave him: in a lordly bowl she brought him cream.

26. She put forth her hand to the pin, and her right hand to strike the weary; she struck Sisera, pierced his head, and wounded and penetrated his temple.

27. At her feet he sank, fell, lay; at her feet he sank (and) fell; where he sank, there he fell down dead.

28. Through the window the mother of Sisera looked forth, and peered through the window; why is his chariot late in coming? Why tarry the strides of his chariots?

29. The wisest of her princesses answer her, she too returns

answers to herself.
30. 'Are they not finding (and) dividing the spoils? A damsel, two damsels to every man; a spoil of dyed garments to Sisera, a spoil of dyed garments of embroidery; dyed garments of embroidery for the neck of the spoiler.'
31. So may perish all Your enemies, O Lord; but they that love Him (should be) as the sun when he goes forth in his might." (Book of Devorah, Chapter 5)

PAINTING ON THE PARSHA

The parsha of Beshallach may be one of the most challenging in our emerging national narrative. We are finally freed from horrific slavery, and yet caught up in corrosive emotions of revenge and sadistic joy in seeing God's creatures annihilated.

In light of that, sometimes we simply need to follow our wise leaders, beyond the carnage and into the challenges of embracing our awesome God. (R.M.)

Moses and Aaron Leading the People by Richard McBee

> The Torah's description of the Song at the Sea is curious in that it actually presents two songs; one led by Moses, possibly for the men alone and one led by Miriam for all the women. Perhaps the female version was filled with joy and celebration for we are told the women danced with musical instruments, whereas the men forcefully expresses the full scope of the devastation of the Egyptian army. (R.M.)

Moses and Miriam Sing the Song at the Sea
by Richard McBee

YISRO
CREATIVITY & BOUNDARIES: ALLURE AND DANGER OF APPROACHING THE TRUE BEING

In the *parsha* of Yisro, God commands Moses regarding the setting of boundaries for the Jewish people's assembly at Mount Sinai when they are to receive the Torah (Shemot 18:12-13):

"And you shall set boundaries for the people around, saying, Beware of ascending the mountain or touching its edge; whoever touches the mountain shall surely be put to death.	יב. וְהִגְבַּלְתָּ אֶת הָעָם סָבִיב לֵאמֹר הִשָּׁמְרוּ לָכֶם עֲלוֹת בָּהָר וּנְגֹעַ בְּקָצֵהוּ כָּל הַנֹּגֵעַ בָּהָר מוֹת יוּמָת:
No hand shall touch it, for he shall be stoned or cast down; whether man or beast, he shall not live. When the ram's horn sounds a long, drawn out blast, they may ascend the mountain."	יג. לֹא תִגַּע בּוֹ יָד כִּי סָקוֹל יִסָּקֵל אוֹ יָרֹה יִיָּרֶה אִם בְּהֵמָה אִם אִישׁ לֹא יִחְיֶה בִּמְשֹׁךְ הַיֹּבֵל הֵמָּה יַעֲלוּ בָהָר:

Rashi explains "when the ram's horn sounds a long, drawn-out blast, this is a sign of the *Shechinah's* withdrawal and the cessation of the voice (of God). As soon as the *Schechinah* withdraws, they are permitted to ascend (from Mechilta).

The experiencing of holiness by a person includes both drawing close in certain ways and, at the same time, remaining distant from God. This dual and paradoxical dimension of our relationship with the Creator is expressed throughout our history and within Jewish law. At Mount Sinai, when every Jew was about to experience God in perhaps the most direct manner possible for human beings, great emphasis is placed on the boundaries that were to be strictly adhered to. There is also a curious dialogue between

God and Moses regarding these boundaries. At the point where God is about to give the Torah and the *Aseres Hadibros* (the tablets containing the 10 statements often called "the 10 Commandments") he instructed Moses to go down and warn the people once more to keep to the boundary limitations, as they were instructed previously. The Torah states (Shemot 19:21-25):

The Lord said to Moses, "Go down, warn the people lest they break [their formation to go nearer] to the Lord, and many of them will fall.	כא. וַיֹּאמֶר יְהוָה אֶל מֹשֶׁה רֵד הָעֵד בָּעָם פֶּן יֶהֶרְסוּ אֶל יְהוָה לִרְאוֹת וְנָפַל מִמֶּנּוּ רָב:
And also, the priests who go near to the Lord shall prepare themselves, lest the Lord wreak destruction upon them."	כב. וְגַם הַכֹּהֲנִים הַנִּגָּשִׁים אֶל יְהוָה יִתְקַדָּשׁוּ פֶּן יִפְרֹץ בָּהֶם יְהוָה:
And Moses said to the Lord, "The people cannot ascend to Mount Sinai, for You warned us saying, Set boundaries for the mountain and sanctify it."	כג. וַיֹּאמֶר מֹשֶׁה אֶל יְהוָה לֹא יוּכַל הָעָם לַעֲלֹת אֶל הַר סִינָי כִּי אַתָּה הַעֵדֹתָה בָּנוּ לֵאמֹר הַגְבֵּל
But the Lord said to him, "Go, descend, and [then] you shall ascend, and Aaron with you, but the priests and the populace shall not break [their formation] to ascend to the Lord, lest He wreak destruction upon them."	כד. וַיֹּאמֶר אֵלָיו יְהוָה לֶךְ רֵד וְעָלִיתָ אַתָּה וְאַהֲרֹן עִמָּךְ וְהַכֹּהֲנִים וְהָעָם אַל יֶהֶרְסוּ לַעֲלֹת אֶל יְהוָה פֶּן יִפְרָץ בָּם:
So Moses went down to the people and said [this] to them.	כה. וַיֵּרֶד מֹשֶׁה אֶל הָעָם וַיֹּאמֶר אֲלֵהֶם:

Rashi explains that we learn from this, that a person is warned twice regarding the intention of performing of a violation- once some time before the act and a second time when they are about to perform the act. It seems that there are two states of mind, each requiring a separate warning- one when a person intends to perform a violation and a different state of mind right before the act. For example, someone may plan to murder or steal, but at the point of carrying it out, experience a new type of conflict not present when the planning was for something in the future. At this point, a second warning can be an important obstacle to help the person restrain themselves from the act. But with regards to the second warning given to the people to keep the boundaries at Mount Sinai, we can explore the unique ambivalence regarding boundaries as it relates to "approaching God".

Rabbi Joseph B. Soloveitchik explains in his essay "And From There You Shall Seek" that a human being longs for closeness to God in the most fundamental way because a human being senses that his or her own existence is unreal and temporary and that all true Existence only exists in God. The longing for God is really the longing to truly exist by cleaving to the One, True Existent. The Rav states:

> The metaphysics of the book of redemption (the Book of Exodus) is expressed in the phrase "I am that I am" (Ex. 3:14). I necessarily exist, and wherever you find being, you will discern the illumination of My sole existence. Whenever someone or something "is" in the finite third person, the "I am" of the infinite "I" reveals itself. The "Let there be" of the six days of creation continues to exist because the "I am" of fire in the bush reveals itself from within in it. The Deity is the pure existent that brings everything into existence and encompasses everything….There is no existence without God, and there is no reality without reliance on Him. God therefore draws after Him the creature who yearns for complete existence, who senses the emptiness of his world and dependence of his concrete being. (page 62)

The Jewish people at Mount Sinai were about to have the ability to draw close to God as no others had before.

Perhaps the second warning was necessary from this perspective. Once the people assemble and await the Revelation, they will not be prepared for the unique experience of longing to cleave to God that will occur when they are on the verge of this experience. This experience was unprecedented and unique. Perhaps this was, in part, the nature of the obscure second warning which Moshe was commanded to communicate to them. But the question needs to be asked, why do we need boundaries? Why shouldn't we fully experience the closeness to God to the absolute extent that we can? Why shouldn't the Jewish people approach Mount Sinai without any boundaries at all! The Rav responds to this question in this same essay and explains that intense closeness to God bring with it a sense of the loss of oneself and a type of terror in the realization of one's own nothingness. From this perspective, the setting of boundaries and the warnings are God's acts of protection and caring for the Jewish people who might long so intensely to come too close and be destroyed by the overwhelming experiencing of God's Being. One is reminded of the four great scholars who entered "*Pardes*" (Paradise) with the results being that one died, one lost his faith and one lost his mind. Only Rabbi Akiva remained undamaged and some say that it was because he knew which boundaries to maintain, even while in the "*Pardes*". Otto states:

> The fear of the annihilation of being is interwoven with the yearning for the elevation of being, a yearning that is fulfilled by coming closer to God. The spirit that longs for its divine lover wraps itself around the grandeur of His might. It turns, fades, and disappears into the terrible Infinity that fills everything and surrounds everything, that causes everything and outlasts everything. "You shall set bounds for the people round about, saying 'Beware of going up the mountain or touching the border of it" (Ex. 19:12);…He must not enter the place where the *Shekhinah* is located. One who utters the

holy name of God in vain has transgressed a negative commandment…Sometimes it is necessary for there to be a tension of great fear that is manifested in retreat. God constructs universes and destroys them, says the Midrash (Gen. Rabbah 37). The Tetragrammaton is both a noun and an adjective, and in its adjective form it expresses two ideas: (1) the coming into being of what exists; (2) the annihilation of what exists (pp. 63-64).

The Rav clarifies here that the longing for God that is at the core of our being, is not a longing to know, as much as a longing "to be". On some level we recognize that our existence is not only limited by its length, but by it being something of a "shadow existence", with God being the only True Existent. Yet we long to truly exist and therefore, long to cleave to God. A description of this sense of ourselves as a created, contingent being, sometimes referred to as our "creatureness" (sense of being created and maintained by a true Existent) is focused on in a text by Rudolph Otto, "The Idea of the Holy", which is often referred to by the Rav. Otto explains how this experience can result is a person's overwhelming sense of his or her own nothingness and powerless to a level that would be able to bring on death, madness or apostasy. Otto calls this sense of the True Existent "the numen" (Webster's translates this term as "divine presence") He writes:

> The numen, overpoweringly experienced, becomes the all-in-all. The creature, with his being and doing, his 'willing' and 'running', his schemes and resolves, becomes nothing. The conceptual expression to indicate such a felt submergence and annihilation over against the numen is then-here impotence and there omnipotence; here the futility of one's own choice and there the will that ordains all and determines all….To the creature then is denied, not merely *efficacy* as a cause, but true *reality* and complete being, and all existence and fullness of being is ascribed to the absolute entity, who alone really *is*, while all 'being' of creatures is either a function of this

absolute Being-which brings them into existence-or mere illusion. (The Idea of the Holy, Oxford University Press pp. 89-90)

It is this dangerous approaching of God for one who is not prepared that is behind the boundaries to holiness, which is fundamental to the Jewish system of law and study. Moses was able to approach because his level of perception of himself and the world was such that it would not be destructive to sense God's presence in the most intense manner. Aaron was able to approach closer, but not as close and the *kohanim*, not as close as Aaron, etc. Rashi explains this on the following *pasuk* (Exodus 19:24):

4. But the Lord said to him, "Go, descend, and [then] you shall ascend, and Aaron with you, but the priests and the populace shall not break [their formation] to ascend to the Lord, lest He wreak destruction upon them."	כד. וַיֹּאמֶר אֵלָיו יְהֹוָה לֶךְ רֵד וְעָלִיתָ אַתָּה וְאַהֲרֹן עִמָּךְ וְהַכֹּהֲנִים וְהָעָם אַל יֶהֶרְסוּ לַעֲלֹת אֶל יְהֹוָה פֶּן יִפְרָץ בָּם:
Rashi: and [then] you shall ascend, and Aaron with you, but the priests: I might think that they too shall be with you, [that the verse should be rendered: and you shall ascend, and Aaron with you, and the priests, but the people…]. Therefore, the Torah states: "and you shall ascend" [the pronoun is meant for emphasis, in order to exclude the priests]. Consequently, you must say that you [shall have] a partition for yourself, Aaron [shall have] a partition for himself, and the priests [shall have] a partition for themselves. Moses went closer than Aaron, and Aaron closer than the priests, but the people shall altogether not break their position to ascend to the Lord. — [from Mechilta]	ועלית אתה ואהרן עמך והכהנים: יכול אף הם עמך, תלמוד לומר ועלית אתה. אמור מעתה, אתה מחיצה לעצמך ואהרן מחיצה לעצמו והם מחיצה לעצמם. משה נגש יותר מאהרן, ואהרן יותר מן הכהנים, והעם כל עיקר אל יהרסו את מצבם לעלות אל ה':

Perhaps it is this danger to the self of too intense an experience of God's Being that explains why the other prophets had their contact filtered through the images of dreams and visions. The direct communication to the intellect, according to Maimonides is "passed through" to the imaginative faculty where it is interpreted from the images of the vision or dream. In this indirect way, the person not on Moshe's level can preserve the integrity of their personality through a more moderated contact with the *Ein Sof* (the Infinite).

In Moses' case, he did not view himself or his value in a relative sense, as he had achieved total humility- a humility by which he had come to assess his value relative to the God's infinite Being and therefore direct contact was not damaging to him.

Boundaries for Torah Scholars & Observant Artists

The desire we have to create, both in the intellectual and artistic spheres, are bounded by Jewish law. There are areas of knowledge that Jewish people, with the exception of great scholars, are restricted from exploring. This restriction is regarding the study of areas that are labeled "*Pardes*" and refer to highly fundamental knowledge about the nature of God and creation. We are also to observe restrictions set out in the law to prevent our own intellectual, emotional and spiritual damage. As we have described above, certain knowledge can uproot a person's basic perspective and leave them bereft of any way to maintain their sense of importance, dignity or purpose, if they are not emotionally and intellectually prepared for this knowledge. Maimonides states in the Mishna Torah (Fundamentals of Torah):

> These concepts are extremely deep, and not every [person has] the knowledge necessary to appreciate them. In his wisdom, Solomon described them with the metaphor

[Proverbs 27:26]: "Lambs for your clothing." [The root *kevas* - "lamb" - also has the meaning "hide."] Thus, our Sages interpreted this metaphor [to mean]: Matters which are the secrets of the world will be your clothing - i.e., they will be for you alone, and you should not discuss them in public. Concerning them, [Proverbs 5:17] teaches: "They shall be for you and not for others with you." [Similarly, the Song of Songs 4:11] states: "Honey and milk will be under your tongue." The Sages of the early generations interpreted this [as a metaphor]: Subjects that are like honey and milk should be [kept] under your tongue. (Chapter 2, Halacha 12)

The Observant artist also has boundaries to observe. All of our scholars agree that certain types of artistic creation are not permitted to the Jewish artist. This is a complex area of Jewish law so I will quote from Maimonides Mishneh Torah "Laws of Idolatry" and from Rabbi Abraham Yitzchak Kook, the first chief Rabbi of Israel (before it was a Modern State) who was focused on this area because of his efforts to establish the Betzalel Institute of Arts in the Holy Land.

Maimonides states:

It is prohibited to make images for decorative purposes, even though they do not represent false deities, as [implied by Exodus 20:23]: "Do not make with Me [gods of silver and gods of gold]." This refers even to images of gold and silver which are intended only for decorative purposes, lest others err and view them as deities. It is forbidden to make decorative images of the human form alone. Therefore, it is forbidden to make human images with wood, cement, or stone. This [prohibition] applies when the image is protruding - for example, images and sculptures made in a hallway and the like. A person who makes such an image is [liable for] lashes. In contrast, it is permitted to make human images that are engraved or painted - e.g., portraits, whether on wood or on stone - or that are part of a tapestry. (Laws of Idolatry: 3:10).

The commentator the Tur states in Yoreh De'ah 14- states that we are forbidden to make only a complete human statue.

A bust of a head alone or a statue which is lacking any one of the body's limbs in not forbidden. This opinion is shared by the Ramah. (The Laws of Idolatry 3:10)

Rav Kook states:

> The whole realm of adornment, ornamentation, beautification and painting is permitted to Jews. There is only one limit, one mark, seemingly very long, but distinguished in its quality and not its quantity. This limit conveys much spiritually but does only minimum harm to craftsmanship and art for all the power of its noble purpose. "All visages are allowed, save the face of man" (Talmud, Rosh Hashanna 24b). In fact, only the sculpture of a complete human face (is prohibited) and there are ways of understanding (by which even this prohibition may be circumvented, such as through the help of a gentile assistant in the final stage of a prohibited sculpture. What is left, then is only a small point of the whole long line, but God's designs are manifold, the nation of Israel shall abhor and not bear those pictures specifically characteristic of idolatry, whether of the pagan world of past or present or of the Christian world. (Rav Kook's Selected Letters –Translated and Annotated by Tzvi Feldman. Letter 24)

Below is a poem by Rav Kook that is relevant to the issues discussed in this analysis.

POETRY ON THE PARSHA

Expanses, Expanses by Rav Abraham Yitzchak Kook

Expanses, expanses, expanses divine my soul craves.
Confine me not in cages of substance or of spirit.
My soul soars the expanses of the heavens, walls of heart and walls of deed will not contain it.
Morality, logic, custom –my soul soars above these, above all that bears a name,
Above delight, above every delight and beauty, above all that is exalted and ethereal.
I am love-sick –I thirst, I thirst for God, as a deer for water

brooks.

Alas, who can describe my pain, who will be a violin to express the songs of my grief,

Who will voice my bitterness, the pain of seeking utterance? I thirst for truth, not for a conception of truth, for I ride on its heights,

I am wholly absorbed by truth, I am wholly pained by the anguish of expression.

How can I utter the great truth that fills my whole heart? Who will disclose to the multitude, to the world, to all creatures, to nations and individuals alike,

The sparks abounding in treasures of light and warmth Stored within my soul? I see the flames rise upward piercing the heavens, but who feels, who can express their might?

I am not like one of those heroes who have found whole worlds in their inwardness.

Whether the world knew of their wealth or not, it was all the same to them.

These herds of sheep walking on two feet —for what use was it if they knew man's true height,

And what loss in their not knowing?

I am bound to the world, all creatures, all people are my friends,

Many parts of my soul are intertwined with them,

But how can I share with them my light?

Whatever I say only covers my vision, dulls my light.

Great is my pain and great my anguish, O, my God, my God, be a help in my trouble,

Find for me the graces of expression, grant me language and the gift of utterance,

I shall declare before the multitudes my fragments of Your truth, O my God.

PAINTINGS ON THE PARSHA

Approaching God and resolutely remaining separate…apart. This becomes our conflicted metaphor with the moment and memory of us and the mountain. (R.M.)

Sinai Mountain by Richard McBee

The Jewish people, men and women together, here witness Moses' divine revelation. They are all included by the *chuppah* in the symbolic marriage of the Jewish people with God, and yet Moses' experience is kept singular by the fence surrounding the mount. (R.M.)

Sinai Chuppah by Richard McBee

MISHPATIM
CREATIVITY & SENSITIVITY: WIDOWS, ORPHANS AND THE JUSTICE OF MERCY

In the parsha of Mishpatim, it states (Shemot 22:20-13):

You shall not oppress any widow or orphan.	כא. כָּל אַלְמָנָה וְיָתוֹם לֹא תְעַנּוּן:
If you oppress him, [beware,] for if he cries out to Me, I will surely hear his cry.	כב. אִם עַנֵּה תְעַנֶּה אֹתוֹ כִּי אִם צָעֹק יִצְעַק אֵלַי שָׁמֹעַ אֶשְׁמַע צַעֲקָתוֹ:
My wrath will be kindled, and I will slay you with the sword, and your wives will be widows and your children orphans.	כג. וְחָרָה אַפִּי וְהָרַגְתִּי אֶתְכֶם בֶּחָרֶב וְהָיוּ נְשֵׁיכֶם אַלְמָנוֹת וּבְנֵיכֶם יְתֹמִים:

The Torah gives special consideration and protection to widows and orphans, as stated in these *pasukim*. A number of questions can be asked about this special status:

1- What precisely is the way to fulfill the mitzvah of *lo taanoon* ("do not oppress") - how does one violate this prohibition?

2- Why is a separate mitzvah needed to prohibit oppression of the widow and orphan when there is already a mitzvah of *"v'ahavta rayecha kmoecha"* (that you should love your fellow as you do yourself)? Certainly, if one must love his fellow, he cannot oppress him!

3- Why does the Torah state the punishment for violating this prohibition as God "slaying you with the sword, and your wives will be widows and your children orphans"? God does not use weapons such as swords and isn't it obvious that the person's death will leave his children as orphans and his wife as a widow? What does this add?

Maimonides states in the Mishnah Torah, *Hilchos Dayot* (*Laws of Character Traits 6:10*)

> A person is obligated to show great care for orphans and widows because their spirits are very low and their feelings are depressed. This applies even if they are wealthy. We are commanded to [show this attention] even to a king's widow and his orphans as [implied by Exodus 22:21]: "Do not mistreat any widow or orphan." How should one deal with them? One should only speak to them gently and treat them only with honor. One should not cause pain to their persons with [overbearing] work or aggravate their feelings with harsh words and [one should] show more consideration for their financial interests than for one's own. Anyone who vexes or angers them, hurts their feelings, oppresses them, or causes them financial loss transgresses this prohibition. Surely this applies if one beats them or curses them.

For one's fellow Jew, the obligation is not identical with that of a widow or orphan, as Maimonides states in *Hilchot Dayot* (*Laws of Character Traits 6:3*)

> Each man is commanded to love each and every one of Israel as himself as [Leviticus 19:18] states: "Love your neighbor as yourself." Therefore, one should speak the praises of [others] and show concern for their money just as he is concerned with his own money and seeks his own honor.

A widow or orphan is treated with *extreme sensitivity* and not with the level of concern that one would expect from others for oneself. The guiding point of reference for how to treat a fellow Jew is how one expects himself to be treated. Every emotionally healthy person has a fairly clear sense of what is means for him to be treated with kindness and concern. All that is required for understanding how to treat a fellow Jew is for a person to reflect on one's own standard of how he or she would expect to be treated and to apply that to the other people that he interacts with. Maimonides does give basic guidelines in this halacha quoted above, stating "Therefore, one should speak the praises of [others] and show concern for their money just as he is concerned with his own money and seeks his own honor." In my opinion this is not exhaustive and the halacha's reference to monetary and honor-related actions as they are ones often violated when people interact with each other.

Returning to the widows and orphans, a Jew who interacts with them is at much greater risk of causing them pain and anguish. It is extremely difficult for a person to be sensitive to feeling that he or she does not have. A person who has a healthy sense of security and a reasonably secure ego, is not bothered by what he considers minor slights or insensitivities in the way people talk or act with him. It is like a person who cannot feel the pressure of an extremely light object on his hand. It is as if it does not exist for him. So how is this person to muster the sensitivity in his interactions with the widow or orphan who does feel these minor slights as considerable pain and anguish due to what Maimonides described earlier in the Mishneh Torah as *spirits are very low and their feelings are depressed*? I believe our response to this question will clarify two of the questions we asked earlier – why a separate halacha for the widows and orphans?; why does the Torah use such a dramatic description of the punishment (that God will slay the person with a sword and make his children orphans and his wife a widow?).

In order for the average person to achieve the level of sensitivity necessary not to oppress the very sensitive natures of the widow and the orphan, he must be highly motivated to concentrate on the situation of these unfortunate individuals. God often motivates a person with fear. But stating such a severe punishment for a seemingly minor mistake, the person is made to understand that extreme caution must be taken with them in order to protect one's own life. It reminds me of how a person would act in the presence of a king, where one minor insult could result in immediate death or imprisonment. This is the attitude that the description of God "slaying the person with a sword" brings to mind. But perhaps a more subtle and effective method of aiding the person in keeping this law is the description that "your wives will be widows and your children orphans". This image, when reflected on by the potential oppressor, helps him put himself in the place of the widow or orphan and feel something of what they are feelings. Although the average person's imagination cannot naturally sense the pain of widows or orphans, the average person CAN imagine the pain of his own wife or children if they were in such a situation. This imagining allows for a heightened sensitivity in the person that is needed in order to properly fulfill this mitzvah.

I would like to pose the question, whether treating the widow and orphan with such "extra" sensitivity is an act of justice or an act of mercy. One might assess this to be a merciful act, since it goes beyond the standard manner of concern with which one treats his fellow and expects to be treated by others. But perhaps the special treatment afforded the widow and orphan is not mercy, but simply justice. For these individuals, the extreme level of sensitivity is what they require to function properly. Their situation is like a baby who can only eat soft food. Is it mercy for the parent to give the baby soft food because the parent can eat hard food? I don't think so. It is simple justice. So too, the widow and orphan, in light of their depressed and insecure state, require the "soft food" of extreme kindness to survive and thrive.

Sensitivity and Compassion in the Torah Scholar and the Observant Artist

The analytic and intense personality that is well-suited to achieved advanced Torah scholarship is not necessarily one that is naturally compassionate and sensitive to others. Rabbi Joseph B. Soloveitchik ("the Rav") would often speak of how his grandfather Rav Chaim Soloveitchik had worked just as diligently on developing his sensitivity towards others, as he did on his development as a Torah scholar. Through this effort Rav Chaim Soloveitchik achieved a legendary level of concern and compassion for the most vulnerable. Rav Chaim Bagley stated in a *yartzeit shiur* for Rav Chaim Soloveitchik:

> One Shabbos morning in 1910, I joined my father at Reb Chaim's private minyan in his house. We noticed a baby carriage in the living room and Reb Chaim seemed very concerned. The child was not Reb Chaim's own, but one that was left abandoned at his doorstep. (It was widely known that a child that would not have a normal upbringing for one of any number of reasons would find a warm welcome in Reb Chaim's home.) (matzav.com)

Maimonides also states quite emphatically, the centrality of helping the oppressed and the unparalleled joy one receives from it in his work, the Mishneh Torah, when clarifying the laws of the Purim:

> It is better for a person to increase gifts to the poor (" במתנות "אביונים) rather than to increase the '*seudah*' or the '*m'shloach manot*' because there is no greater or more glorious joy than to bring joy to the hearts of the poor, the orphans, the widow and the converts. To bring joy to these people in misery is similar to the '*Shechinah*' as it states: "To revive the spirit of the fallen and to revive the heart of the crushed." (Laws of Purim 2:16)

To my understanding, there is a great struggle for the Torah scholar to develop the compassion and sensitivity to the poor and vulnerable that is required and lauded by the Torah. There are contrary elements to the persona that achieves scholarly success and that of the sensitive individual. A scholar must be focused in youth on his or herself almost exclusively to develop the skills and knowledge required to achieve mastery. This requires ignoring others and cultivating scholarly self-absorption. Also, the scholar is often driven by a competitive, aggressive personality which, at least initially, is quite antithetical to the sensitivity towards widows, orphans and other vulnerable individuals required by the Torah. Most scholars go through, what I would call, a "fledgling period" when they exhibit these somewhat narcissistic and cruel tendencies. It is only with the "seasoning of age" and the inculcating of the Torah's absolute valuing of sensitivity, kindness and compassion for the downtrodden, that the great scholar, like Rav Chaim Soloveitchik, becomes a deeply compassionate person. Many do not achieve this level, and their scholarship is tainted and, to a great extent, distorted, by their own sense of superiority and greatness. It is instructive to note that Moses, the greatest of the Torah scholars and prophets, is also described by the Torah as the humblest of people. This humility, I would suggest, was achieved through Moses assessing himself as a mere servant of God and, as such, without a sense of greatness, due to his continual awe of the Creator's perfection. It is only when one measure's one's worth in comparison with other people that a scholar can be filled with a sense of greatness and superiority, which can often lead to an insensitivity towards others.

The observant artist's personality may have sensitivities to certain aspects of the world, beyond that of their peers. But this sensitivity often does not lead to an individual that is compassionate and sensitive to others feelings. This is not the artists' "medium": and in many cases, the opposite in true.

The observant artist, as any artist, is focused on the creative process. This is usually a focus on the skillful and sensitive manipulation of words, paints, music or some other medium, to achieve an intended effect, and the communication of an inner perspective, thought or feeling. It is true that an artist needs to have a sensitivity to how his or her art will impact the person experiencing the artistic creation (e.g., the listener, viewer, reader, etc.) But this is a highly limited area of sensitivity and does not often extend to the sphere of compassion and kindness to those in need. The artist's desire to create is an intensely personal and individual experience. When absorbed in the intense act of creating, all other concerns, such as those of the family, community and needy, can easily be forgotten. Also, the artist often possesses a strong sense of the importance of his or her work. This perception that the creation of their art fulfilling an important personal "destiny" can justify a profoundly selfish existence. In a sense, artists can see the creation of their art as so important, that's its creation justifies the ignoring of the problems of the poor and other in need of assistance.

As with the Torah scholar, the observant artist has no "*heter*" (leniency) that allows him or her to ignore other requirements as a Jew and human being. We do not have the concept in Judaism of people who are involved in so exalted an activity, that they are relieved of their duties of compassion, kindness and assistance. The observant artist or Torah scholar cannot utilize the "logic" that their being involved in a great creative undertaking removes or diminishes their obligations as compassionate human being. Taking this to the next level, it would seem that, when possible, a Torah scholar or observant artist should attempt to utilize their creativity and talents to relieve the suffering of those who are vulnerable and in need. Whether their creativity can be utilized to bring attention to, or to work towards, solutions to the suffering of the misfortunate, this application of their talents would be aligned with their obligations as Jews and members of the community. Many artists have used their works to bring attention to issues of cruelty and injustice within the community and have used their creativity to help "repair the world" ("*tikkun olam*"). The observant artist must strike a balance between the solitary and self-absorbed process of artistic creation and the obligation we all have to utilize our talents and energies to address the needs of those in need.

Below is a selection from Yishayahu (Isaiah) and poems relevant to the current discussion.

History by Charles Simic (From "Unending Blues")

Men and women with kick-me signs on their backs.
Let's suppose he was sad and she was upset.
They got over it. The spring day bore a semblance to what they hoped.
Then came History. He was arrested and shot.
Do they speak in heroic couplets as he's dragged away looking over his shoulder?
A few words for that park statue with pigeons on it?
More likely she wipes her eyes and nose with a sleeve,
Asks for a stiff drink, takes her place in the breadline.
Then the children die of hunger, one by one.
Of course, there are too many such cases for anyone to be underlining them with a red pencil.
Plus, the propensity of widows to flaunt their widowhood:
Course pubic hair, much-bitten breasts.
History loves to see women cry, she whispers.
Their death makes Art, he shouts, naked.
How pretty are the coffins and instruments of torture
In the Museum on the day of free admission to the public!

The Chimney Sweeper (From "Songs of Innocence")
by William Blake

When my mother died I was very young, and my father sold me while yet my tongue
Could scarcely cry " 'weep ! 'weep ! 'weep ! 'weep ! so your chimneys I sweep, & in soot I sleep.
There's little Tom Dacre, who cried when his head, that curl'd like a lamb's back, was shav'd: so I said
"Hush, Tom ! never mind it, for when your head's bare
You know that the soot cannot spoil your white hair."
And so he was quiet, & that very night, as Tom was a-sleeping, he had such a sight ! ---
That thousand of sweepers, Dick, Joe, Ned, & Jack, were all of them lock'd up in coffins of black.
And by came an Angel who had a bright key, and he open'd the coffins & set them all free;
Then down a green plain leaping, laughing, they run, and wash in a river, and shine in the Sun.
Then naked & white, all their bags left behind, they rise upon clouds and sport in the wind;
And the Angel told Tom, if he'd be a good boy, he'd have God for his father, & never want joy.
And so Tom awoke; and we rose in the dark, and got with our bags & our brushes to work.
Tho' the morning was cold, Tom was happy & warm; so if all do their duty they need not fear harm.

Yishayahu (Isaiah) Chapter 1:

| 11. Of what use are your many sacrifices to Me? says the Lord. I am sated with the burnt-offerings of rams and the fat of fattened cattle; and the blood of bulls and sheep and he goats I do not want. | יא. לָמָּה לִּי רֹב זִבְחֵיכֶם יֹאמַר יְהֹוָה שָׂבַעְתִּי עֹלוֹת אֵילִים וְחֵלֶב מְרִיאִים וְדַם פָּרִים וּכְבָשִׂים וְעַתּוּדִים לֹא חָפָצְתִּי: |

12. When you come to appear before Me, who requested this of you, to trample My courts?

יב. כִּי תָבֹאוּ לֵרָאוֹת פָּנָי מִי בִקֵּשׁ זֹאת מִיֶּדְכֶם רְמֹס חֲצֵרָי:

13. You shall no longer bring vain meal-offerings, it is smoke of abomination to Me; New Moons and Sabbaths, calling convocations, I cannot [bear] iniquity with assembly.

יג. לֹא תוֹסִיפוּ הָבִיא מִנְחַת שָׁוְא קְטֹרֶת תּוֹעֵבָה הִיא לִי חֹדֶשׁ וְשַׁבָּת קְרֹא מִקְרָא לֹא אוּכַל אָוֶן וַעֲצָרָה:

14. Your New Moons and your appointed seasons My soul hates, they are a burden to Me; I am weary of bearing [them].

יד. חָדְשֵׁיכֶם וּמוֹעֲדֵיכֶם שָׂנְאָה נַפְשִׁי הָיוּ עָלַי לָטֹרַח נִלְאֵיתִי נְשֹׂא:

15. And when you spread out your hands, I will hide My eyes from you, even when you pray at length, I do not hear; your hands are full of blood.

טו. וּבְפָרִשְׂכֶם כַּפֵּיכֶם אַעְלִים עֵינַי מִכֶּם גַּם כִּי תַרְבּוּ תְפִלָּה אֵינֶנִּי שֹׁמֵעַ יְדֵיכֶם דָּמִים מָלֵאוּ:

16. Wash, cleanse yourselves, remove the evil of your deeds from before My eyes, cease to do evil.

טז. רַחֲצוּ הִזַּכּוּ הָסִירוּ רֹעַ מַעַלְלֵיכֶם מִנֶּגֶד עֵינָי חִדְלוּ הָרֵעַ:

17. Learn to do good, seek justice, strengthen the robbed, perform justice for the orphan, plead the case of the widow.

יז. לִמְדוּ הֵיטֵב דִּרְשׁוּ מִשְׁפָּט אַשְּׁרוּ חָמוֹץ שִׁפְטוּ יָתוֹם רִיבוּ אַלְמָנָה:

PAINTINGS ON THE PARSHA

Justice can of course take many forms; financial, physical and even mental. And yet the Torah's extreme sensitivity for the widow, orphan and the exposed seems to emphasize a cleaving, i.e. an embrace of one person with another. When the Shunemite woman protested to Elisha the death of her beloved son, she threw herself down and grasped his legs, refusing to leave until the shocked prophet would properly address her problem. (R.M.)

Elisha and the Shunemite Woman by Richard McBee

Similarly Ruth refused to be sent back to her homeland. Instead she embraced her mother-in-law, pledging fealty to her life, her people and her God. (R.M.)

Naomi and Ruth by Richard McBee

TERUMAH
CREATIVITY AND THE SANCTUARY

In the parsha of Terumah God commands Moshe regarding the specific forms and materials required for the construction of the Sanctuary (*mishkan*) and its vessels. The Torah states:

8. And they shall make Me a sanctuary and I will dwell in their midst	ח. וְעָשׂוּ לִי מִקְדָּשׁ וְשָׁכַנְתִּי בְּתוֹכָם:
And they shall make Me a sanctuary: And they shall make in My name a house of sanctity.	ועשו לי מקדש: ועשו לשמי בית קדושה:
9. according to all that I show you, the pattern of the Mishkan and the pattern of all its vessels; and so shall you do.	ט. כְּכֹל אֲשֶׁר אֲנִי מַרְאֶה אוֹתְךָ אֵת תַּבְנִית הַמִּשְׁכָּן וְאֵת תַּבְנִית כָּל כֵּלָיו וְכֵן תַּעֲשׂוּ:
Rashi: according to all that I show you: here, the pattern of the Mishkan. This verse is connected to the verse above it: "And they shall make Me a sanctuary…" according to all that I show you.	ככל אשר אני מראה אותך: כאן את תבנית המשכן. המקרא הזה מחובר למקרא שלמעלה הימנו ועשו לי מקדש ככל אשר אני מראה אותך:
10. They shall make an ark of acacia wood, two and a half cubits its length, a cubit and a half its width, and a cubit and a half its height.	י. וְעָשׂוּ אֲרוֹן עֲצֵי שִׁטִּים אַמָּתַיִם וָחֵצִי אָרְכּוֹ וְאַמָּה וָחֵצִי רָחְבּוֹ וְאַמָּה וָחֵצִי קֹמָתוֹ:

Our scholars have differed regarding whether the commandment to build a sanctuary (*mishkan*) was part of the "ideal" Torah system or whether it was an "addendum", so to speak, added to the Torah as a necessary response to the Jewish people's lower level of holiness as a result of their creation of the Golden Calf. The 17th century Italian scholar Ovadiah ben Yoseph Sforno held that the sanctuary was a concession to the damage caused by this violation. But for this catastrophe, according to Sforno, a Sanctuary would not have been necessary. He writes:

> Finally God clarified matters when he said: "Make Me a sanctuary for Me to dwell in", a step he had not originally contemplated. Previously He had been satisfied with: "Make me an altar of earth...wherever I make mention of My name I will come to thee". But henceforth he required priests and this He announced when He said: "As for thee bring near to thee Aaron thy brother". The tribe of Levi was not chosen to minister until after the incident of the Golden Calf.

Yitzchak ben Yehudah Abarbanel, a 15th century Portuguese scholar, views the Golden Calf as the cause of all Torah laws given to the Jews regarding the Sanctuary and sacrifices ("*avodah*"). He states:

> At the beginning God did indeed only command Israel in civil but not sacrificial laws. But after they made the golden calf and He observed their sinful ways and moral weaknesses He was constrained to provide an antidote for their spiritual infirmity. The sacrifices filled this function, each type for particular offences and weaknesses. They would not have been commanded to sacrifice had they not sinned. (commentary on Yermiyahu 7:22-23).

The creating of a "dwelling place" for God seems to be contrary to the fundamental principle that God does not have a body nor a location where He would actually "dwell". So the establishment of the Mishkan and the holy objects within it, is somewhat misleading in that it might imply that God "locates" Himself at certain coordinates at certain times.

Maimonides famously characterized the Temple and the sacrificial service as a concessionary in his "Guide for the Perplexed", Maimonides concludes that the concession was due to the historical development of the Jewish people from an idolatrous world in which temples and sacrifice were the established methods of worship. Torah, which had come to "repair the world" ("*tikkun haolam*") needed to elevate the Jewish people, utilizing the practices and concepts which had been established historically, and to wean them away from idolatrous misconceptions by repairing these concepts. To have removed the sacrificial ritual completely at the point when the Torah was given, was, according to Maimonides, not feasible. He states:

> ...and as at that time the way of life generally accepted and customary in the whole world and the universal service upon which we were brought up consisted in offering various species of living beings in the temples in which images were set up, in worshipping the latter, and in time, as we have explained, the people who were devoted to the service of the temples consecrated the stars-: His wisdom, may He be exalted, and His gracious plan, which is manifest in regard to all His creatures, did not require that He give us a Law prescribing the rejection, abandonment, and abolition of all these kinds of worship. For one could not then conceive the acceptance of (such a Law) considering the nature of man, which always likes that to which it is accustomed....Therefore He, may He be exalted, suffered the above mentioned kinds of worship to remain, but transferred them from created or imaginary and unreal things to His own name, may He be exalted. Thus He commanded us to build a temple for Him: *And let them make Me a Sanctuary, (Exodus 25:8)* to have an altar for His name: *An altar of earth thou shalt make unto Me, (Exodus 20:24)* to have the sacrifice offered up to Him: *When any man of you brings an offering unto the Lord (Leviticus 1:2)*,

Nachmanides ("the Ramban") did not view the Sanctuary as a concession. He explains the command of the Sanctuary as preceding the Golden Calf incident and as being included as an optimal part of the Torah system. The Ramban views the Sanctuary as a type of recreation of Mount Sinai and, just as God's glory rested among the Jewish people on the mountain when they received the Torah, it would continue to "reside" with them in the Sanctuary. He states:

The secret of the Tabernacle is that the Glory which abode upon Mount Sinai (openly) should abide upon it in a concealed manner. For just as it said there, *And the glory of the Eternal abode upon Mount Sinai (Exodus 24:16)* and it is further written, *Behold, the Eternal our God has shown us His glory and His greatness, (Deuteronomy 5:21)* so it is written of the Tabernacle, *and the glory of the Eternal filled the Tabernacle (Exodus 40:34)*.

The Holiness of the Sanctuary

The differences of opinion regarding whether the Sanctuary was required as a necessary response to the Golden Calf, or whether its inclusion in the Torah system was unrelated to this event, does not detract from the holiness that the Torah system assigns to it. All Torah scholars agree that the land of Israel is the holiest land and the city of Jerusalem, the holiest city. Within the city, the Temple was the holiest place, and within it, the Holy of Holies (*Kadshey Kadashim*) which contained the ark (*aron*), was the holiest of the Sanctuary's sections (See Mishnah Keilim 1:6). The concept of holiness and its meaning has been discussed often by our scholars and in our previous analyses. Rabbi Joseph B. Soloveitchik ("the Rav") in his essay, "The Emergence of Ethical Man", ascribes to the view that the holiness of the land is attributable to its historical role in the formation of the Jewish people and how the awareness of this history impacts the mind and soul of the individual. He states:

> *Kedushah (RB-"holiness")*, under halakhic aspect, is man-made; more accurately, it is a historical category. A soil is sanctified by historical deeds performed by a sacred people, never by any primordial superiority. The halakhic term *kedusha-ha-aretz*, the sanctity of the land, denotes the consequence of a human act, either conquest (heroic deeds) or the mere presence of the people in that land (intimacy of man and nature). *Kedushah* is identical with man's association with Mother earth. Nothing should be attributed a priori to dead matter. Objective *kedusha* smacks of fetishism. (The Emergence of Ethical Man, 151)

As the Rav sees it, the holiness of the land of Israel is due to the cluster of acts by which God and man interacted meaningfully in that place, and not through some inherent force within the physical matter. Holiness is bestowed upon the place, according to the Rav, because of its history of consequential events, not due to any inherent spiritual power that resides within the physical land. The Rav's statement about the land would seem to be equally true of the Temple and the Sanctuary, as the Mishnah cited in *Keilim* includes both the land of Israel, the city of Jerusalem and the areas of the Temple among the 10 levels of holiness. The offering of Isaac on Mount Moriah was also the place where Jacob laid his head and dreamed his prophetic "ladder dream". This location would become the sight of the Temple in the future.

In addition to holiness being due to the history of a location, the Torah clarifies that this quality can adhere to a place or an object due to the activity that is performed in that place or with that object. The Sanctuary in the desert and the Temple in Jerusalem were places of service or servitude *(avodah)* to the Creator. These places and objects had no other designation and were strictly proscribed from any other use. For this reason an object, such as a Torah scroll or *tefillin*, also possess a degree of holiness which is reflected in the laws of their restricted use. As a general rule, the holier an object, the more restrictions that are placed on its use. Maimonides explains the efficacy of this structure in his work "The Guide for the Perplexed" in relation to the extreme restrictions regarding those who were permitted to enter the Sanctuary:

> We have already explained that the intention with regard to the Sanctuary was to cause those that came to it to experience feelings of awe and of reverence; as it says: *You shall fear My Sanctuary (Leviticus 19:30)*. Now if one in continually in contact with a venerable object, the impression received from it in the soul diminishes and the

feeling it provokes becomes slight. The sages, may their memory be blessed, have already drawn attention to this notion, saying that it is not desirable that the Sanctuary should be entered at every moment, and in support quoted its dictum: *Let thy foot be seldom in thy neighbor's house, lest he be sated with thee, and hate thee.* This being the intention, He, may He be exalted, forbade the unclean to enter the Sanctuary in spite of there being many types of uncleanness, so that one could-but for a few exceptions-scarcely find a clean individual. (Book 3: Chapter 47).

Creativity and the Making of the Sanctuary

I would like to briefly explore the nature of the act of constructing the *Mishkan* and its contents. Was the building of the Sanctuary and the formation of its holy objects an artistic act, or would they perhaps fall more accurately under the heading of construction and production? After all, the Torah in Shemot 25:9 clearly states that Moshe was instructed by God to make the sanctuary and its objects in a specified manner which was provided:

according to all that I show you, the pattern of the Mishkan and the pattern of all its vessels; and so shall you do.	ט. כְּכֹל אֲשֶׁר אֲנִי מַרְאֶה אוֹתְךָ אֵת תַּבְנִית הַמִּשְׁכָּן וְאֵת תַּבְנִית כָּל כֵּלָיו וְכֵן תַּעֲשׂוּ:

Was there more involved here than the following of a blueprint with precision and accuracy? We are told in the Torah that Betzalel, the master building of the Sanctuary and its contents, was a person of great talent, skill and inspiration, but it is not clear whether this refers to his level of technical skill, or whether he contributed creatively to the final form. The Torah states:

1. The Lord spoke to Moses, saying:	א. וַיְדַבֵּר יְהוָה אֶל מֹשֶׁה לֵּאמֹר:
2. "See, I have called by name Bezalel the son of	ב. רְאֵה קָרָאתִי בְשֵׁם בְּצַלְאֵל בֶּן אוּרִי בֶן

Uri, the son of Hur, of the tribe of Judah,	חוּר לְמַטֵּה יְהוּדָה:
3. and I have imbued him with the spirit of God, with wisdom, with insight, with knowledge, and with [talent for] all manner of craftsmanship	ג. וָאֲמַלֵּא אֹתוֹ רוּחַ אֱלֹהִים בְּחָכְמָה וּבִתְבוּנָה וּבְדַעַת וּבְכָל מְלָאכָה:
4. to do master weaving, to work with gold, with silver, and with copper,	ד. לַחְשֹׁב מַחֲשָׁבֹת לַעֲשׂוֹת בַּזָּהָב וּבַכֶּסֶף וּבַנְּחֹשֶׁת:
5. with the craft of stones for setting and with the craft of wood, to do every [manner of] work.	ה. וּבַחֲרֹשֶׁת אֶבֶן לְמַלֹּאת וּבַחֲרֹשֶׁת עֵץ לַעֲשׂוֹת בְּכָל מְלָאכָה:

Interestingly, God states that Betzalel has been "imbued with wisdom (*chuchma*), with insight (*tevunah*) and with knowledge (*daat*). These three distinct intellectual abilities are qualities possessed by Betzalel, it seems, in addition to the ability to do "all manner of craftsmanship" in the various craft techniques. Far from being simply a master craftsman or engineer, our commentators have ascribed to Betzalel the highest level of metaphysical knowledge. The creation of the Sanctuary has been paralleled by our rabbis with the creation of the Earth itself and Betzalel viewed as being endowed with a unique, esoteric creative ability that mirrored, in some way, God's creation of the Earth.

Naftali Zvi Yehuda Berlin (The "Netziv"), a 19th century Torah scholar and Rosh Yeshiva of the Volozhin Yeshiva writes:

> "In wisdom, and in understanding, and in knowledge." It has already been explained (*Shemot* 25:8) that all of the worlds were included in the building of the Mishkan and

its vessels. For this reason, the *Shekhina* rested within it, as it was at the beginning of the creation, when the *Shekhina* oversaw His world in general. Just as the world in general was created with these three attributes, as it is written: "The Lord by wisdom founded the earth; by understanding He established the heavens. By his knowledge the depths were broken up" (*Mishlei* 3:19-20) – in this way the *Mishkan* had to be built with these three attributes, and similarly the *Mikdash* in which the *Shekhina* would rest. And this is what we find in *Midrash Rabba* that Betzalel knew how to join together the letters with which heaven and earth were created. Thus is explained the words, "And I have filled him with the spirit of God," this word sometimes meaning that He created heaven and earth, as I have written at the beginning of *Parashat Bereisheit* (1:1) and in other places.

Rabbi Shimshon Raphael Hirsch, the great 19th century German scholar, views Betzalel's construction of the sanctuary as the ultimate example of human craft and artistry in which man "changes this earthly world into a home for the kingdom of God". As such, the construction of the Sanctuary become the Torah's paradigm for human creative work and that work which had to cease in celebration of the Sabbath. Rav Hirsch states:

> The building of the *Mishkan*, if not from the point of view of art, still surely from the point of view of the idea and the purpose to be realized by the idea of "And let them make Me a sanctuary, that I may dwell among them" (*Shemot* 25:8), is the very highest conceivable plan for human artistic activity. The mastery of man over matter, in getting, producing, changing, and manufacturing the raw materials of the world, attained its highest meaning in the Temple. The world submits to man, for him to submit himself and his world to God and for him to change this earthly world into a home for the kingdom of God, to a Temple in which the glory of God tarries on earth. The building of the Temple is a sanctification of human labor, and in the context here, it is represented as being a combination of all those creative activities of man, by the

cessation of which, by resting from all labor, the Sabbath is made into an acknowledgment of man's allegiance to God. Each kind of activity which came to be used for the building of the Temple is made thereby into a major category (*av*) of forbidden labor, which includes many creative activities of the same basic idea, as derivatives (*tolada*) of that idea. For instance, sowing and planting is an *av*, a category of productive activities, under which are listed activities such as pruning trees, watering plants, and all acts of furthering growth, as *toledot* (see *Shabbat* 73b). As our text limits the penalty of "whoever does work on it shall be put to death" to "the words which the Lord has commanded," and then stresses "that you should do them," the intention must be not only to do the act, but also to do them; the intention must be to produce the actual result of the action. Only productive, not destructive activities constitute the idea of work, and only provided it is neither unintended nor not needed for its own sake is it considered the full desecration of Sabbath, regarding which it says "whoever does work on it shall be put to death." In all cases, reference to the work of the *Mishkan* is considered.(*Shemot* 35:2)

The Mishkan, the Artist and the Scholar

We view here, a rare example of the Torah focusing on the interplay and cooperation of the greatest prophet in Moshe with the supreme artisan and craftsman in Betzalel. The following midrash depicts a fascinating event regarding the creation of the Sanctuary's menorah and how Betzalel's was able to create it even though Moshe, with direct instruction from God, was unable to do so. The midrash states:

> Rabi Levy the son of Rebi said: Hashem explained to Moshe how to make the Menorah. However, it was too difficult for him to grasp. Moshe came back to Hashem a second time, and Hashem actually showed him how to go about it, but again it was too hard for him. Hashem then created an image of the Menorah out of fire and showed it to Moshe, but Moshe still could not understand how to implement the vision. Finally, Hashem told Moshe to go to Betzalel who would know how to make it. Moshe went to

> Betzalel, who created it on the spot. Moshe was shocked. How could you, Betzalel, who never saw the image and who received no instruction from Hashem, create what I could not grasp?" (Midrash (Tanchuma -Behaalotcha 6)

Although the midrash does not reveal precisely what were the abilities that Betzalel had that allowed him to succeed where Moshe could not, it is certainly instructive in showing that there is an aspect of deep Torah insight which is within the sphere of the arts that is necessary to "allow" God to dwell among us. There is some degree of validation, it seems, from this intriguing encounter, of the productive wedding of scholarship and the arts. Moshe, the greatest scholar is called upon to be the artisan and Betzalel, the greatest artisan, is portrayed as one of the great scholars, possessing of the highest and most esoteric knowledge of God.

In conclusion I would like to suggest that the greatness of Betzalel in understanding God was necessary for his creating of the Mishkan and its objects, to assure that he would carefully restrain from "crossing the fine line" through which the Mishkan could have become a source of idolatry. Although the patterns and structures were provided by God, perhaps the nuance of its execution, left to the builder, could turn out to be the difference between the perfect "concession" to man's need for a positioned focus of his worship and the false idea of God having a physical dimension. For this reason, Betzalel needed wisdom, understanding and knowledge of the highest degree and a complete mastery of all crafting skills.

POETRY ON THE PARSHA

Below is a selection of poems that are relevant to our discussion:

In the Paths of the Ark by Yehudah Halevi

Turn aside with me to Zoan, to the Red Sea, to Mount Horeb.
I will go round unto Shiloh to the heap of the ruined shrine,
And will get me along the paths of the Ark of the Covenant,
Until I taste the dust of its hiding place that is more sweet than honey,
And I see the habitation of that beauteous one who hath forgotten her nest,
Since the doves be driven away and ravens abide there.

Because of this my soul is sorely sick and grieved,
For through my sin the morn is turned to evening time.
Verily my heart faints and longs for the mount of myrrh,
Even as the soul desires to find its innermost home.

Excerpt from "Jerusalem, Jerusalem, Why Jerusalem?
by Yehuda Amichai

Longing for Jerusalem, for childhood in Jerusalem, in another faraway time:
The children of the Levites longing, now that they are old, in exile by the water of Babylon.
They still remember singing in the Temple when their voices had just begun to change.
At night they remind one another of their childhood;
'Remember how we played hide-and-seek behind the Holy of Holies, among the urns of frankincense, near those drainage ditches around the altar, in the shadow of the embroidered mantle on the Holy Ark, between the cherubim?'

Jerusalem, Port City by Yehuda Amichai

Jerusalem, Port City of the shore of forever.
The Temple Mount a great ship, a splendid pleasure boat.
From the portholes of her Western Wall smiling saints look out.
They are travelers. Hasidim wave greetings from the pier, shouting *hurrah, au revoir.* She's always arriving, always leaving. And walls and wharfs and guards, and flags and tall masts of churches and mosques and chimney of synagogues and boats of praise and mountain waves. The sound of the shofar; one more has set out. Yom Kippur sailors in white uniforms climb on ladders and ropes of tested prayers.

On a Night of Rain in Jerusalem by Uri Zvi Greenberg

The few trees in the yard moan like a forest. The thunderous clouds are heavy with rivers. The Angels of Peace stand at the head of my sleeping children, as the trees moan and the heavy rains pour down.

Outside: Jerusalem, city of the Father's glorious trail, when he bound his son on one of the hills. That fire, kindled at dawn, still burns on the hill, the rains have not put it out: it is the fire between the sacrificial pieces.

'If God were to command me now, as once He did my ancient Father, I would surely obey,' sing my heart and my flesh on this night of rain, as the Angels of Peace stand at the head of my sleeping children!

What can equal this glory, this wondrous zeal-alive since that ancient dawn to this moment-for the Mount of Moriah? The blood of the covenant sings on in the father's fervent body. He is prepared to offer his sacrifice on the Temple Mount as dawn.

Outside: Jerusalem, and the moaning of the Lord's trees, cut down by her enemies in every generation; clouds heavy with rain, lightning's in them and thunders which for me, on this night of rain, are tidings from the mouth of the God of Might to endless generations.

PAINTINGS ON THE PARSHA

Creativity and the Sanctuary

Archie Rand imagines the portable Tabernacle as a remarkably simple affair; an schematic aerial view of a ramped sacrificial altar and a little two-part house containing the holy menorah, its steps, the showbread table and a tiny altar, all residing outside a mysterious Holy of Holies. (R.M.)

Terumah – by Archie Rand

In late 13th century Perpignan the illuminator arranged the sanctuary implements schematically on facing pages, loosely divided into those used in the courtyard on the left as opposed to those used inside the Holy on the right. Each utensil is clearly labeled, even objects that are not explicitly mentioned in the text, such as the little stairs to facilitate lighting the rather tall menorah. Not surprisingly the cherubim are positioned above the ark containing the tablets of the law with the first words of the 10 commandments inscribed. (R.M.)

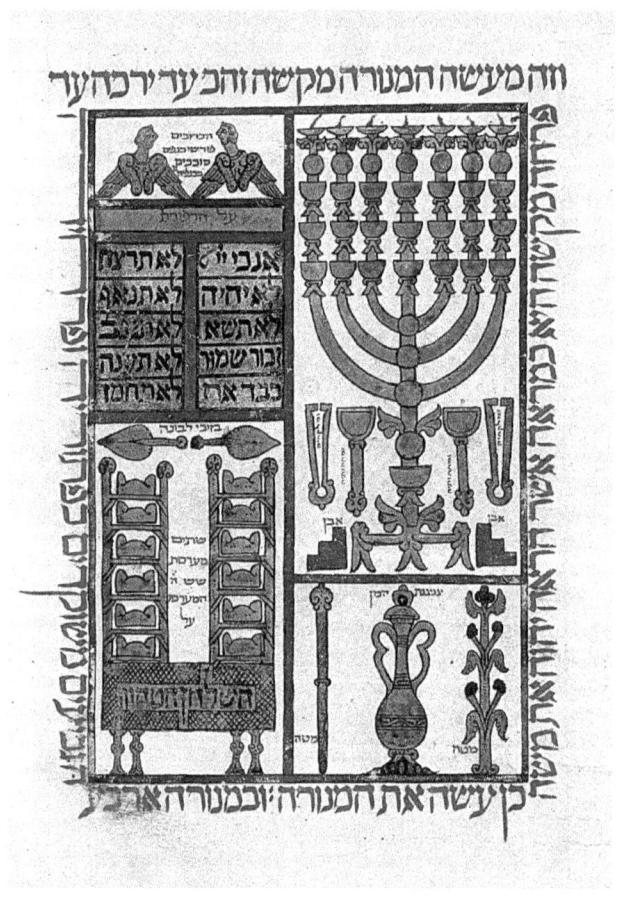

13th Century Perpignan Manuscript

One leaf from the British Museum's Miscellany (1280) provides a figurative depiction of Aaron supplying oil for the menorah, one of many depictions of the human figure in medieval Jewish texts. The manuscript may have been created in Troyes, France and the Gothic grace and style of the figure suggests influence from contemporary Christian manuscripts. (R.M.)

13th Century British Museum Miscellany

It is fairly certain that many of the depictions of the implements of the Tabernacle express a messianic yearning for the redemption from exile and restoration of the Temple. Tragically, the most famous depiction expresses the opposite perspective. The Roman Arch of Titus, created in 85 CE to celebrate the destruction of the Temple and defeat of the Jewish commonwealth, depicted the golden menorah, fire pans, silver trumpets and the Shewbread Table triumphantly carried into Rome. According to Josephus the actual menorah was kept in Rome in Vespasian's nearby Temple of Peace until the Ostrogoth Sack of Rome in the 5th century when it disappeared. Little could he or the many medieval illuminators who depicted the menorah have guessed that it would become the symbol of the reborn State of Israel in the 20th century. (R.M.)

Arch of Titus, Rome

TETZAVEH
CREATIVITY, PRIESTLY ROBES & THE HUMAN IMAGE

The *parsha* of Tetzavah describes the special clothing to be created for the Kohanim (priests). (Exodus 28:2-3).

2. You (Moshe) shall make holy garments for your brother Aaron, for honor and glory.	ב. וְעָשִׂיתָ בִגְדֵי קֹדֶשׁ לְאַהֲרֹן אָחִיךָ לְכָבוֹד וּלְתִפְאָרֶת:
3. And you shall speak to all the wise-hearted, whom I have filled with the spirit of wisdom, and they shall make Aaron's garments to sanctify him, [so] that he serve Me [as a kohen].	ג. וְאַתָּה תְּדַבֵּר אֶל כָּל חַכְמֵי לֵב אֲשֶׁר מִלֵּאתִיו רוּחַ חָכְמָה וְעָשׂוּ אֶת בִּגְדֵי אַהֲרֹן לְקַדְּשׁוֹ לְכַהֲנוֹ לִי:
Rashi: to sanctify him, [so] that he serve Me [as a kohen]: Heb. לְקַדְּשׁוֹ לִי-לְכַהֲנוֹ, to sanctify him, to initiate him into the kehunah through these garment [so] that he would be a kohen to Me. The expression of kehunah means service, serjanterie [or serventrie] in Old French.	לקדשו לכהנו לי: לקדשו להכניסו בכהונה על ידי הבגדים שיהא כהן לי, ולשון כהונה שירות הוא, שוריינטריא"ה בלעז [שירות]:

The Torah which is often brief in its description of details, leaving many specifics of the Torah laws to be expounded in the oral tradition, is exceptionally specific in the case of the priestly garments. The 8 pieces of the *Kohane Gadol's* (the High Priest's) ornate garb are described by the Torah in great detail. The *Kohane's* donning of these garments is absolutely essential for him to carry out his function. If he lacks any one of them he is subject to the punishment given to a non-*Kohane* that carries out the priestly services. This Torah obligation is described in the Sefer HaHinnuch under Commandment 99: "the precept that Kohanim should wear their special garments"):

> Now, as long as any *kohane*, an ordinary one or the *kohane gadole*, serves in less than (the proper number) of his garments that were expressly for that service, or in more than them, his service is disqualified; and moreover, he incurs death at the hands of Heaven-as our Sages of blessed memory derived the ruling from the verse "And you shall gird them with sashes...and the *kahunah* (the position of kohane) shall be theirs.

The Talmud explains:

> If one serves as a priest without the full priestly raiment, one's service is disqualified. At the time their raiment is upon them their priesthood is upon them. If their raiment is not upon them, their priesthood is not upon them. (Talmud Bavli, 17b)

Also of interest is the fact that Aaron - not Moses-was selected by God to be the *Kohane Gadole* and that Moshe was commanded to dress Aaron and his sons in their priestly robes. The Torah states:

8. And you (Moshe) shall bring his sons near, and you shall clothe them with tunics.	ח. וְאֶת בָּנָיו תַּקְרִיב וְהִלְבַּשְׁתָּם כֻּתֳּנֹת:
9. And you shall gird them with sashes, Aaron and his sons, and you shall dress them with high hats, and the kehunah will be a perpetual statute for them, and you shall invest Aaron and his sons with full authority.	ט. וְחָגַרְתָּ אֹתָם אַבְנֵט אַהֲרֹן וּבָנָיו וְחָבַשְׁתָּ לָהֶם מִגְבָּעֹת וְהָיְתָה לָהֶם כְּהֻנָּה לְחֻקַּת עוֹלָם וּמִלֵּאתָ יַד אַהֲרֹן וְיַד בָּנָיו:

The midrash Shemot Rabbah 37:4, in an intriguing and cryptic statement, describes God's "passing over" of Moshe for the role of Kohane Gadole, comparing the situation to a husband telling his barren wife to go seek for him a wife who can bear him children. The midrash states:

> And as for you, you shall bring forward your brother Aaron…(Exodus 28:1). It is written, "If Your Torah had not been my plaything, I should have perished in my poverty" (Ps 119:92). When God told Moses, "As for you, you shall bring forward your brother Aaron…" He did him an injury. God said, "I had possession of the Torah, and I gave it to you: if it were not for the Torah I should have lost My world!" This is like a wise man who married his relative and after ten years together, when she had not borne children, he said to her, "Seek me a wife!" He said to her, "I could marry without your permission, but I seek your cooperation." So said God to Moses, "I could have made your brother High Priest without informing you, but I wish you to be great over him."

In this analysis I would like to explore the following questions:

1-Why were the *kohane's* garments so essential to his status and the performance of his duties?
2-Why were Aaron selected, instead of Moses, to serve as the Kohane *Gadole*?

In addressing these two questions I hope we can gain some insight regarding the Jewish law restricting the creation of human images. Why is the prohibition on creating decorative images limited to only the human figure? I would like to try to support the idea that the worship of the human being (self-worship) is at the root of human idolatrous thought and activity.

The Uniform and Human Individuality

Uniforms are specific garments that often identify and honor a person's role within a group. The uniform shifts the focus from the person's individual self to an emphasis on the person's place and role within the collective. The most prominent example of this phenomenon is the use of the uniform in the military. Here the uniform takes on great importance and is an absolute requirement for the soldier with punishments given to one who fails to wear or maintain his or her uniform properly. In part, the uniform serves to create a greater cohesiveness among the group and a sense of belonging and responsibility to the other members of that group.

This idea is relevant to the *kohane* as well. The *kohane* was afforded great respect and privilege according to Jewish law and even today, the *kohane* is called to the Torah first and asked to lead in the grace after meals, when he is present. In the time of the Temple, the *Kohane Gadole* (the high priest) was greatly loved and honored by the Jewish people, more so than any other individual in the society. Maimonides clarifies in the "Guide for the Perplexed" the honor shown the high priest, as well as the reason why the death of the *Kohane Gadole* released those exiled to the Cities of Refuge. He states:

> In order to raise the estimation of the Temple, those who ministered therein received great honor; and the priests and Levites were distinguished from the rest. It was commanded that the priests should be clothed properly with beautiful and good garments, "holy garments for glory and for beauty" (Exodus 28:2). A priest that had a blemish was not allowed to officiate; and not only those that had a blemish were excluded from the service, but also-according to the Talmudic interpretation of this precept-those that had an abnormal appearance; for the multitude does not estimate man by his true form but by

> the perfection of his bodily limbs and the beauty of his garments, and the Temple was to be held in great reverence by all. (Book 3, Chapter 44).

Regarding the release of those accidental murderers who were exiled to the City of Refuge upon the death of the *Kohane Gadole*, Maimonides states:

> The chance of returning from exile depends of the death of the high-priest, the most honored of men, and the friend of all Israel. By his death the relative of the slain person becomes reconciled for it is a natural phenomenon that we find consolation in our misfortune when the same misfortune or a greater one has befallen another person. Amongst us no death causes more grief that that of the high priest. (Book 3, Chapter 40).

To my mind, the risk of idolatry to the Jewish people is most pronounced with regards to the *Kohane Gadole*. As the most honored and holiest of the Jewish people, as well as the one who approaches God in the most intimate manner, he was at risk of being worshipped as a god or an intermediary. Only the *Kohane Gadole* enters the Holy of Holies on Yom Kippur to supplicate for the Jewish people's forgiveness. An individual's great desire to draw close to God can tempt one to embrace the human being as some form of god-like being. In Egypt the pharaoh was worshipped as a god-man. This idea was also at the root of the Greek and Roman pantheon of gods. The idolatrous desire takes a most pronounced form in the Christian religion where the basis of their faith holds that God took human form. Although there are many animal and tree -derived idols, these too, I believe have their root in human traits that are transfigured into animal and tree forms. Strength, size, productivity, fertility, etc. which have their value as human traits are expressed in an animal form in these idols, but it is man's fantasies of immortality and omnipotence that serve as the psychic source for all these idolatrous thoughts and activities. For example, the golden calf did not attract the Jewish people in the desert because of an inordinate love of cattle, but because the calf had certain traits that represented human qualities or human situations that were intensely satisfying to the people, whether fertility, strength, obedience, etc.

It seems plausible that the system of Torah that so vigilantly guards against idolatry would create the position of *Kohane Gadole* in a manner to prevent him from achieving a god-like quality in the eyes of the people, though still retaining the great respect and honor that was required to bring honor to the Temple as the focal point of God's presence on Earth and its holiest place. In line with this agenda, Moses would be excluded from the *Kohane Gadole* position. There is a valid "concern" by God that the people would worship Moses. We see a hint of this in the fact that Moses was buried by God and that the location of Moses' grave was not revealed to anyone. This can be viewed as preventing the people from creating a shrine at his grave. (Devarim 34:6)

| And He buried him in the valley, in the land of Moab, opposite Beth Pe'or. And no person knows the place of his burial, unto this day. | ו. וַיִּקְבֹּר אֹתוֹ בַגַּי בְּאֶרֶץ מוֹאָב מוּל בֵּית פְּעוֹר וְלֹא יָדַע אִישׁ אֶת קְבֻרָתוֹ עַד הַיּוֹם הַזֶּה: |

Rashi quotes the Talmud Sotah 14a on this verse, that "God, Himself buried Moses". Moses' greatness in the eyes of the people was too great to be the *Kohane Gadole* as well, as this may have led to his being worshipped as a god-man. By "distributing" the greatness to Aaron, God dissipated Moses' greatness in the eyes of the people as it was now shared between the two.

The primacy of the garments in the role of the *Kohane* also, I believe, diminishes the likelihood that the *Kohane Gadole* would become an object of worship. As stated earlier, the uniform diminishes the importance of the individual and raises up his greatness as a member of the collective. The *Kohane Gadole's* greatness, as represented in his garments, is related to his place within the Jewish people. Without them he is without glory and greatness. God's greatness is independent of his people or any of his creations. This is not so with the *Kohane Gadole*. A general or admiral, once stripped of his uniform and rank, is a mere person with no exalted power. In this way, the garments of the *Kohane Gadole*, while bringing to him greater honor and respect, make it clear that his greatness derives from the office he holds in serving God and the Jewish people and not from something within him that is innate and immortal.

There are other aspects of the *Kohane Gadole* and the regular *Kohanim* that proscribe against their becoming objects of worship. These include:

The golden show-plate *("tzitz zahav")* which was a gold band placed prominently on the head of the *Kohane Gadole* at the base of the turban had the words "Holy to the Lord" which made clear that the *Kohane Gadole* was a possession of God and not a god himself. The Torah states:

36. And you shall make a show plate of pure gold, and you shall engrave upon it like the engraving of a seal: "Holy to the Lord."	לו. וְעָשִׂיתָ צִּיץ זָהָב טָהוֹר וּפִתַּחְתָּ עָלָיו פִּתּוּחֵי חֹתָם קֹדֶשׁ לַיהוָה:
37. And you shall place it upon a cord of blue wool and it shall go over the cap, and it shall be opposite the front side of the cap.	לז. וְשַׂמְתָּ אֹתוֹ עַל פְּתִיל תְּכֵלֶת וְהָיָה עַל הַמִּצְנָפֶת אֶל מוּל פְּנֵי הַמִּצְנֶפֶת יִהְיֶה:

38. It shall be upon Aaron's forehead, and Aaron shall bear the iniquity of the holy things that the children of Israel sanctify, for all their holy gifts. It shall be upon his forehead constantly to make them favorable before the Lord.	לח. וְהָיָה עַל מֵצַח אַהֲרֹן וְנָשָׂא אַהֲרֹן אֶת עֲוֹן הַקֳּדָשִׁים אֲשֶׁר יַקְדִּישׁוּ בְּנֵי יִשְׂרָאֵל לְכָל מַתְּנֹת קָדְשֵׁיהֶם וְהָיָה עַל מִצְחוֹ תָּמִיד לְרָצוֹן לָהֶם לִפְנֵי יְהוָה:

Also, fundamental to the role of the *kohanim* was the bringing of the animal, grain and spice offerings to God. In addition to the sacrifices of the people, the *kohanim* would also have to bring their own sacrifices to God. Again, although they were exalted by the people, it was plain to see that their work was one of service. This service was strenuous and of a highly physical nature, depicting their servitude to God. Unlike other religions where holy men would sit in tranquil contemplation "on a mountain", the holiest of the Jews "worked" for God and the Jews and worked in a way that displayed a servile attitude in the slaughter and burning of the sacrifices.

Restrictions on Creating the Human Image

Regarding Jewish law's specific focus on the formation of human image (complete human statue) being prohibited we will quote from Maimonides "Mishneh Torah: Laws of Idolatry". He explains that the creation of an idol of any type is prohibited (Halacha 9), but with regards to the creation of a decorative object, it is only a three dimensional complete image of the human that is proscribed.

> **Halacha 9**
> A person who has a false god made for himself - even though he, himself, did not actually fashion it, nor worship it - is [punished by] lashing, as [Exodus 20:5] states: "Do not make for yourself an idol or any representation." Similarly, a person who actually fashions a false god for others, even for idolaters, is [punished by] lashing, as

[Leviticus 19:4] states: "Do not make molten gods for yourselves." Accordingly, a person who actually fashions a false god1for himself receives two measures of lashes.

Halacha 10

It is prohibited to make images for decorative purposes, even though they do not represent false deities, as [implied by Exodus 20:23]: "Do not make with Me [gods of silver and gods of gold]." This refers even to images of gold and silver which are intended only for decorative purposes, lest others err and view them as deities. It is forbidden to make decorative images of the human form alone. Therefore, it is forbidden to make human images with wood, cement, or stone. This [prohibition] applies when the image is protruding - for example, images and sculptures made in a hallway and the like. A person who makes such an image is [liable for] lashes. In contrast, it is permitted to make human images that are engraved or painted - e.g., portraits, whether on wood or on stone - or that are part of a tapestry.

POETRY ON THE PARSHA

Simeon The High Priest (excerpt) by Simeon ben Sira (2nd Century B.C.E.)

Chief among his brethren and pride of his people, Simeon son of Yohanan the priest,
In whose time the House was repaired and in whose days the Temple was fortified.
In whose days the wall was built, with battlements to secure the King's palace.
In whose time a reservoir was dug, a cistern thundering with water like the sea.
He safeguarded his people from marauders and strengthened his city against siege.

How glorious he was as he looked out from the Tent of the Presence,

As he emerged from the curtained shrine!
Like a star shining through the clouds, or the full moon on feast days.
Like the sun glittering on the King's palace or the rainbow seen in the cloud.
Like the blossom on the bough at spring time, or a lily by a flowing stream.
Like a flower of Lebanon on a summer's day, or the fire of frankincense upon the offerings.
Like a spreading olive-tree laden with fruit, or an oleaster whose branches drink their fill.
Like a golden vessel in the house of nobleman, encrusted with precious jewels.

Attendants of the Innermost Chamber by Anonymous
(Piyyut from 4th through 7th Century Palestine under Byzantine Rule)

You who are crowned in grandeur, who are wreathed in crowns,
Who celebrate the Most High with hymns of jubilation.
Now glorify the maser of the flame,
For you are stationed within the very heart of the Shekinah.
In the innermost glory of the chamber of chambers.
He has exalted your names above those of His other servants.
He has singled you out from among the servants of the chariot.
Whoever mentions any of you by name-fire consumes him, flames surround him,
Torches whirl about him and glaring coals, coals of wind, coals of splendor shower upon him!

On the Day of Atonement by Yehuda Amichai

On the Day of Atonement in 1967, I put on my dark holiday suit and went to the Old City of Jerusalem.
I stood for some time, before the alcove of an Arab's shop, not far from Damascus Gate.
A shop of buttons and zippers and spools of thread in all colors, and snaps and buckles.
A glorious light and a great many colors like a Holy Ark with its doors ajar.

I told him in my heart that my father too, had such a shop of threads and buttons.
I explained to him in my heart all about the tens of years and the reasons and the circumstances because of which I am now here and father's shop is in ashes there, and he is buried here.

By the time I had finished, it was the hour of 'the locking of the Gates'.
He too pulled down the shutter and locked the gate, and I went back home with all the worshippers.

PAINTINGS ON THE PARSHA

Dura Europos Synagogue Mural (ca235 CE)

The enormous image of Aaron, identified as such in Greek, perhaps for the benefit of non-Jewish visitors, is presiding over the sacrifices on the right and left. The five figures may very well represent his four sons and an Israelite on the lower left who is also allowed to perform the sacrificial act of slaughter. The "Tabernacle" contains the *aron* (holy ark) seen in the doorway with the golden menorah prominently placed before it. This schematic representation of the tabernacle conflates symbolically the temporary desert tabernacle with the permanent Temple alluding to the fervently hoped for final Third Temple. An image of the distant past and hope for the future. (R.M.)

Botticelli (1483) The High Priest and the Purification of the Leper

The leper has just been cured and the High Priest declares him clean, perhaps a typology of the resurrection. Note the bells on the High Priest's hemline. (R.M.)

Domenico Tiepolo (ca. 1800) - Priests and the Lame Man

Just healed, the thankful man is entering into Solomon's porch accompanied by the Kohanim wearing their distinctive hats and robes hemmed with small bells. (R.M.)

**Aaron Wolf Herlingen of Gewitsch (1725)
Haggadah (title page detail)**

Part of the rebirth of Jewish manuscript illumination in the 18th century, this typical title page features Moses and Aaron in ritual garb, echoing similar Christian images. (R.M.)

**Aaron: Cohen Gadol - Monumental Sculpture: Milan
Artist unknown (19th century)**

Note the head plate with the inscription, "Holy to Hashem."

KI TISSA
CREATIVITY, THE GOLDEN CALF AND NATURAL LAW

The parsha of Ki Tissa includes the pivotal and tragic event of the Golden Calf in which Aaron, at the urging of a portion of the Jewish people, creates a golden statue in the form of a calf, when the people miscalculated that Moses had not returned on time from his ascent onto Mount Sinai after 40 days had passed. The Torah states:

1. When the people saw that Moses was late in coming down from the mountain, the people gathered against Aaron, and they said to him: "Come on! Make us gods that will go before us, because this man Moses, who brought us up from the land of Egypt we don't know what has become of him."

א. וַיַּרְא הָעָם כִּי בֹשֵׁשׁ מֹשֶׁה לָרֶדֶת מִן הָהָר וַיִּקָּהֵל הָעָם עַל אַהֲרֹן וַיֹּאמְרוּ אֵלָיו קוּם | עֲשֵׂה לָנוּ אֱלֹהִים אֲשֶׁר יֵלְכוּ לְפָנֵינוּ כִּי זֶה | מֹשֶׁה הָאִישׁ אֲשֶׁר הֶעֱלָנוּ מֵאֶרֶץ מִצְרַיִם לֹא יָדַעְנוּ מֶה הָיָה לוֹ:

2. Aaron said to them, "Remove the golden earrings that are on the ears of your wives, your sons, and your daughters and bring them [those earrings] to me."

ב. וַיֹּאמֶר אֲלֵהֶם אַהֲרֹן פָּרְקוּ נִזְמֵי הַזָּהָב אֲשֶׁר בְּאָזְנֵי נְשֵׁיכֶם בְּנֵיכֶם וּבְנֹתֵיכֶם וְהָבִיאוּ אֵלָי:

3. And all the people stripped themselves of the golden earrings that were on their ears and brought them to Aaron.

ג. וַיִּתְפָּרְקוּ כָּל הָעָם אֶת נִזְמֵי הַזָּהָב אֲשֶׁר בְּאָזְנֵיהֶם וַיָּבִיאוּ אֶל אַהֲרֹן:

4. He took [them] from their hand[s], fashioned it with an engraving tool, and made it into a molten calf, upon which they said: "These are your gods, O Israel, who have brought you up from the land of Egypt!"

ד. וַיִּקַּח מִיָּדָם וַיָּצַר אֹתוֹ בַּחֶרֶט וַיַּעֲשֵׂהוּ עֵגֶל מַסֵּכָה וַיֹּאמְרוּ אֵלֶּה אֱלֹהֶיךָ יִשְׂרָאֵל אֲשֶׁר הֶעֱלוּךָ מֵאֶרֶץ מִצְרָיִם:

Most people who seek a miraculous revelation of God's providence and are quite sure that they would be strengthened to an unshakeable faith by virtue of it, are quite perplexed by the seeming descent of the Jewish people to idolatry so quickly after experiencing the wonders of plagues, the splitting of the sea and the other miracles of the desert. How could this be? However, according to our tradition there is quite a spectrum of perspectives regarding what precisely occurred here with the Golden Calf and whether it actually was idolatry. We will explore Rashi, Ibn Ezra and the Ramban as well as the commentary of Rabbi Aryeh Dessler in the current analysis. This will lead us into a discussion of the question of whether natural law exists (laws of nature) or whether they are an illusion created by God to allow us to operate with free will, but that in reality all events are the direct, unmediated effect of God's direct intervention. We will contrast Rabbi Dessler's view with that of Maimonides as expressed in his "Guide for the Perplexed".

The violation of idolatry is a complex one. Maimonides includes 51 *mitzvot*, (49 negative and 2 positive) in his Mishneh Torah's introduction to this set of laws. Among the major categories of the idolatry laws are the prohibition against creating an idol, as well as the prohibition against worshiping an idol in either the 4 standard ways (bowing, slaughtering an animal, bringing a burnt offering or libations) or worshipping it in any of the specific manners customary to a specific idol. Maimonides expresses the centrality of the prohibition of idolatry in the Torah. He states in the Mishneh Torah:

> The commandment [forbidding] the worship of false gods is equivalent to all the mitzvot, as [implied by Numbers 15:22]: "Lest you err and not perform all the mitzvot...." The oral tradition teaches that the verse refers to the worship of false gods. Thus, we learn that anyone who

acknowledges a false god denies the entire Torah in its totality, all the works of the prophets, and everything that has been commanded to the prophets from Adam, [the first man,] until eternity, as [Numbers 15:23] continues: "...from the day God issued His commandments and afterwards, for your future generations." [Conversely,] anyone who denies the worship of false gods acknowledges the entire Torah in its totality, all the works of the prophets, and everything that has been commanded to the prophets from Adam, [the first man,] until eternity. [This acknowledgement] is fundamental to all of the mitzvot. (Laws of Idolatry 1:4)

According to Rashi, quoting the Talmud, those Jews involved in the Golden Calf incident were culpable of some degree of idolatry. As he comments on the verse:

1. When the people saw that Moses was late in coming down from the mountain, the people gathered against Aaron, and they said to him: "Come on! Make us gods that will go before us, because this man Moses, who brought us up from the land of Egypt we don't know what has become of him."	א. וַיַּרְא הָעָם כִּי בֹשֵׁשׁ מֹשֶׁה לָרֶדֶת מִן הָהָר וַיִּקָּהֵל הָעָם עַל אַהֲרֹן וַיֹּאמְרוּ אֵלָיו קוּם ׀ עֲשֵׂה לָנוּ אֱלֹהִים אֲשֶׁר יֵלְכוּ לְפָנֵינוּ כִּי זֶה ׀ מֹשֶׁה הָאִישׁ אֲשֶׁר הֶעֱלָנוּ מֵאֶרֶץ מִצְרַיִם לֹא יָדַעְנוּ מֶה הָיָה לוֹ:
Rashi: that will go before us: [אֲשֶׁר יֵלְכוּ לְפָנֵינוּThe word יֵלְכוּis in the plural form.] They desired many deities for themselves. - [from Sanh. 63a]	אשר ילכו לפנינו: אלהות הרבה איוו להם:
Rashi: who brought us up from the land of Egypt: And directed us the way we should go up [from Egypt]. Now we need gods who will go before us [instead of Moses].	אשר העלנו מארץ מצרים: והיה מורה לנו דרך, אשר נעלה בה, עתה צריכין אנו לאלהות, אשר ילכו לפנינו:

Along these lines we also see the Torah verse later in the chapter where Moses says to God:

31. And Moses returned to the Lord and said: "Please! This people has committed a grave sin. They have made themselves a god of gold.	לא. וַיָּשָׁב מֹשֶׁה אֶל יְהֹוָה וַיֹּאמַר אָנָּא חָטָא הָעָם הַזֶּה חֲטָאָה גְדֹלָה וַיַּעֲשׂוּ לָהֶם אֱלֹהֵי זָהָב:

Of course, there is also the issue that not all or a majority of the Jewish people seemed to have participated in the Golden Calf incident. Upon Moses' return, only 3,000 people were killed by the *Leviim* as a punishment for the Golden Calf. We read in Shemot 32: 27-28

27. He said to them: "So said the Lord, the God of Israel: 'Let every man place his sword upon his thigh and pass back and forth from one gate to the other in the camp, and let every man kill his brother, every man his friend, every man his kinsman.' "	כז. וַיֹּאמֶר לָהֶם כֹּה אָמַר יְהֹוָה אֱלֹהֵי יִשְׂרָאֵל שִׂימוּ אִישׁ חַרְבּוֹ עַל יְרֵכוֹ עִבְרוּ וָשׁוּבוּ מִשַּׁעַר לָשַׁעַר בַּמַּחֲנֶה וְהִרְגוּ אִישׁ אֶת אָחִיו וְאִישׁ אֶת רֵעֵהוּ וְאִישׁ אֶת קְרֹבוֹ:
Rashi: So said the Lord, the God of Israel: Now, where did He say [this]? "He who slaughters [a sacrifice] to the gods shall be destroyed" (Exod. 22:19). So it was taught in the Mechilta.	כה אמר וגו': והיכן אמר, (שמות כב יט) זובח לא-להים יחרם, כך שנויה במכילתא:
his brother: [i.e.,] from his mother, who was an [ordinary] Israelite [and not a Levite]. -[from Yoma 66b]	אחיו: מאמו והוא מישראל:

28. The sons of Levi did according to Moses' word; on that day some three thousand men fell from among the people.	כח. וַיַּעֲשׂוּ בְנֵי לֵוִי כִּדְבַר מֹשֶׁה וַיִּפֹּל מִן הָעָם בַּיּוֹם הַהוּא כִּשְׁלֹשֶׁת אַלְפֵי אִישׁ:

But in addition, other Jews were punished afterwards by a plague that God brought as a punishment for this incident. Rashi attributes this to those Jews who did not receive warning and therefore could only be executed by God directly. The Torah states:

35. Then the Lord struck the people with a plague, because they had made the calf that Aaron had made.	לה. וַיִּגֹּף יְהוָה אֶת הָעָם עַל אֲשֶׁר עָשׂוּ אֶת הָעֵגֶל אֲשֶׁר עָשָׂה אַהֲרֹן:
Then the Lord struck the people with a plague: [This was] death by the hands of Heaven for [those who sinned in the presence of] witnesses without warning.	ויגף ה' את העם: מיתה בידי שמים, לעדים בלא התראה:

Also, regarding the general population, we can ask the question of how Hur, the son of Miriam, was able to be killed when he tried to stop those from making the Golden Calf? As we read in Rashi on Exodus 32: 5:

> Aaron saw many things. He saw his sister's son Hur, who had reproved them [the Israelites], and they assassinated him.

How would such a thing be possible to carry out – the murder of one of the Jewish people's great leaders- by such as small minority, if there wasn't some degree of acquiescence by a larger part of the population? This murder, Rashi explains, was part of the reason for Aaron's decision to assist in the construction of the Golden Calf.

Also, God says to Moses that he intends to destroy the entire nation and begin again with Moses as the progenitor of a new nation. If the sin was completely confined to this miniscule percentage of the people, why would the destruction of the Jewish people be just or logical? As any society with a "vanguard" or a "fringe group" that expresses extreme ideas or actions, some degree of acceptance by the ruling majority is required or this minority cannot act. We saw this with regards to the Nazis and the German people in modern times and with regards to the Egyptians and the Jewish persecution in ancient times. What a society allows is telling about the true values of a society, even when that which is allowed is done by a small percentage of the society's population.

Ramban & Ibn Ezra-The Golden Calf: Not Idolatry

Avraham Ibn Ezra, an 11th century Spanish commentator states on Shemot 32:1:

> God forbid, God forbid that Aharon should make an idol, or that Israel would want an idol. But they thought that Moshe was dead... When they said "(Make us) Elohim who shall go before us" their intention (by the word 'elohim') was "glory residing in bodily form" (this means, to know the glory of God through reflecting on a form symbolizing the powers of nature-the ambassadors of God, this will be more fully explained later) Thus it was made for the glory of God... But owing to the influence of the mixed multitude...a small number of Israelites thought it was an idol...and said, "these are your gods, O Israel"...The total number of those who worshipped the Calf as an idol was no more than three thousand.

As I understand the Ibn Ezra, there was a violation with the Golden Calf that was perpetrated by a significant part of the Jewish people, but it was not that of idolatry (performing acts of worship service to anything other than God). The violation was, as Ibn Ezra states it, to "know the glory of God through reflecting on a form symbolizing the powers of nature". This was not worship and not the creation of an idol, but was a significant lowering of the level of the Jewish people's worship and understanding of God, and not aligned with their original intended purpose as God's people. For this reason, one could conclude, God sought to destroy them as they could no longer fulfill their original purpose.

Nachmanides, another great 11th century Spanish commentator, also holds that the Jewish people's involvement in the Golden Calf incident did not violate the actual prohibition of idolatry, however he disagrees with Ibn Ezra's conclusions. His commentary is quite difficult to understand. The Ramban states:

> However (Ibn Ezra's) explanation does not seem right to me. The calf was not made in pursuance of the science of planetary influences, so that glory should reside in its form…but their purpose in making that form was to concentrate on its meaning by means of its service; and I have already explained the secret of the first journey.

The Ramban stated in his commentary on regarding this "first journey" (Yeshaya 63:14):

> It is quite true that it is in the manner of the verse, 'He brings forth His glorious arm at Moshe's right hand'; but not as he (Ibn Ezra) understands it. The verse also writes: So You led Your people to make Yourself a *shem tiferet* (a name of glory).

At this point I would like to draw heavily on the commentary and insights of Rabbi Eliyahu Dessler, who tries to clarify the difference between the positions of the Ibn Ezra and the Nachmanidies (Ramban). Rabbi Dessler was the leader of the Gateshead Kollel in England and also served as the *mashgiach ruchani* (spiritual counselor and lecturer on ethical issues) in the Ponevezh Yeshiva in Bnei Brak, Israel in the 1940's. He remains a highly influential and widely read author in areas of Jewish ethics and philosophy and his *Michtav Eliyahu* has been translated into English in the popular "Strive for Truth" texts.

Rabbi Dessler's Rejection of Natural Causation

Rabbi Dessler gives a fascinating explanation regarding the differences in the positions of the Ibn Ezra and the Ramban with regards to the nature of the Golden Calf. Although both commentators, he concurs, do not see the Golden Calf as actual idolatry, they differ as to what was the nature of the lowering of the Jewish people's level through this incident. Rabbi Dessler understands the Ibn Ezra as seeing the Calf as a lowering of the Jewish people level from a miraculous connection to God to one more natural, in that they feared that without Moses' presence they would not be able to maintain their previous high level of closeness to God. Rabbi Dessler states:

> It is well known that at Mt. Sinai the people of Israel were on an extremely high spiritual level, the level of meriting revelation of the *Shechina*; and their affairs were conducted by God on the level of open miracle. But when they realized that they were no longer sure of Moshe's return, they thought they could no longer maintain that high level. Without the Divine aid that was channeled to them through the presence of Mosheh, they felt they were in danger of falling into the hands of the *yetzer*, and as soon as they had succumbed once, there was not limit to the depths to which they could fall. They therefore decided to descend to a more natural level of existence, where they would learn the presence of God from nature itself. ...This is certainly very far from idolatry. According to the halacha there is nothing wrong in making the form of a snake, or a calf, provided it is not for the purpose of worship. The only images it is forbidden to make under any circumstances are the human form, and all four hayyot or the Heavenly Chariot, i.e.-man, lion, ox, eagle-together. (The Golden Calf: Strive for Truth, Part 3).

Rabbi Dessler views Ibn Ezra as citing the error of the Jewish people in descending from the level of maintaining a direct connection to God through open miracle, to one embracing the lower level of drawing close to God through the exploration of the created natural order. The Golden Calf was some form of aid to this latter approach. It was this lowering of their level that was the error and the cause of their potential destruction by God.

But most interesting is Rabbi Dessler's understanding of the Ramban's cryptic commentary on the Golden Calf and what he sees as the reason for the Ramban's disagreement with Ibn Ezra. Rabbi Dessler states:

> Ibn Ezra understands that the wish was to involve themselves in a more natural lifestyle, which at the same time learning that God alone does everything, nature being no more than an instrument in His hands. To this the Ramban objects: "The Calf was not made in pursuance of the science of planetary influence...but to concentrate on its meaning by means of its service." In other words, they made it as a means of attaining the highest level at which a person acts in the world, knowing all the time that there is no reality in his actions. (ibid)

In Rabbi Dessler's opinion, the Ramban differed with Ibn Ezra in that the Ramban holds that the Golden Calf was not brought as an aid to help the people focus on God through the observance of the created natural order, but as an aid to maintaining the highest level which Rabbi Dessler expresses as "knowing all the time that there is no reality in his (man's) actions". What Rabbi Dessler makes clear in this essay, and what he attributes to the Ramban position, is that natural causation is an illusion and a destructive one. To Rabbi Dessler's understanding, man is provided with the illusion of causation - that his acts are relevant to the outcomes of his physical existence, solely to create a situation by which the free will can operate and a human being can acquire reward or punishment. Rabbi Dessler states:

> The highest level of recognition of God is when a person engages in natural physical activities, recognizing the whole time that all he achieves comes from God above. But here, too, there are two possibilities. We have written elsewhere about the man at the keyhole who sees a pen writing, and who has only to open the door to see the person holding the pen. He illustrates one who sees only natural forces operating. When the door of truth is opened, he sees that in reality it is God who acts, holding nature like a pen in His hand. But there is a still higher level: that is, the one who sees that it is not accurate to compare natural causes to a "pen" in the hand of a writer. The pen is, after all, a necessary implement without which the writer cannot perform his task; while God does not require natural causes, neither does He make use of them. His will suffices to carry out all that He wishes. The fact that we see natural causes operating simply means that there is something wrong with our eyesight. (ibid)

In the opinion of Rabbi Dessler, the natural cause is an illusion created by God for the purpose of man's development. This would be similar to a parent who creates a situation by which a young child is made to think that he or she is in charge of the family's baby to teach the child responsibility and concern for the baby, while in reality the parents are controlling everything and making sure the baby is properly cared for and safe. Rabbi Dessler states:

> The Torah obliges each one of us to carry on our lives by reference to natural causes. Adam's lot "by the sweat of your brow shall you eat bread"-applies to us all. The difference between the two levels just mentioned is this. The person at the lower level, since he believes in the efficiency of natural causes, will find this mitzvah perfectly understandable. On the other hand, the person on the higher level, who realizes the essential unreality of natural causes, finds this mitzvah difficult to understand- a *hoke*

like the mitzvah of the Red Heifer. He knows that Hashem does everything without needing to resort to "causes". His will is the direct cause of all things (except, of course, those things which He has deliberately left to human free will: "All is in the hands of Heaven except for the fear of Heaven") He is aware that there is no logical reason why the effect should follow the cause; the whole system of apparent cause and effect is erected by Hashem to form a background for our moral choices and the exercise of our free will.

To Rabbi Dessler's mind, I believe, both the Ibn Ezra and the Ramban agreed with this point of the illusion of causality but differed as to whether the sin of the Golden Calf was one of trying to maintain this level of understanding by the inappropriate aid of the Golden Calf) (this would be the Ramban's view) or whether the sin involved with the Golden Calf was the lowering of the Jewish people to a level where natural causes are considered effective, thereby distancing themselves from the deeper understanding of the "unreality" of natural causes.

Maimonides, Natural Law and Miracles

My understanding of Rabbi Dessler's position is that everything is directly caused by God and the only distinction between a miracle and non-miracle is whether the event adheres to the structure of the illusion of natural causation which Rabbi Dessler holds God has set up to allow us to exercise our free will. The umbrella over your head does not keep you dry; God's direct intervention makes it so. I do not believe that Rabbi Dessler's view is in agreement with Maimonides (the "Rambam") with respect to causation and natural law. Maimonides states regarding this issue in his "Guide for the Perplexed":

> My opinion on this principle of Divine Providence I will now explain to you. In the principle which I now proceed to expound I do not rely on demonstrative proof, but on

my conception of the spirit of the Divine Law, and the writings of the Prophets. The principle which I accept is far less open to objections, and is more reasonable than the opinions mentioned before. It is this: In the lower or sublunary portion of the Universe, Divine Providence does not extend to the individual members of species except in the case of mankind. It is only in this species that the incidents in the existence of the individual beings, their good and evil fortunes, are the result of justice, in accordance with the words, "for all His ways are judgments." But I agree with Aristotle as regards all other living beings, and a fortiori as regards plants and all the rest of earthly creatures. For I do not believe that it is through the interference of Divine Providence that a certain leaf drops (from a tree), nor do I hold that when a certain spider catches a certain fly, that this is the direct result of a special decree and will of God in that moment; it is not by a particular Divine decree that the spittle of a certain person moved, fell on a certain gnat in a certain place, and killed it; nor is it by the direct will of God that a certain fish catches and swallows a certain worm on the surface of the water. In all these cases the action is, according to my opinion, entirely due to chance, as taught by Aristotle. Divine Providence is connect Divine intellectual influence, and the same beings which are benefited by the latter so as to become intellectual, and to comprehend things comprehensible to rational beings, are also under the control of Divine Providence, which examines all their deeds in order to reward or punish them. It may be by mere chance that a ship goes down with all her contents, as in the above-mentioned instance, or the roof of a house falls upon those within; but it is not due to chance, according to our view, that the men went into the ship, or remained in the house in the other instance. It is due to the will of God, and is in accordance with understanding. (Book 3: Chapter 16)

Maimonides position is that there is causation and natural law operating at all times and in all situations on Earth except with regards to the human being. This exception for human beings is due to God's providential intervention (outside of natural law) being reserved for those being that are intelligent. The Rambam continues:

> Why should God select mankind as the object of His special Providence, and not other living beings? For he who asks this question must also inquire, 'Why has man alone, of all species of animals, been endowed with intellect?'...I hold that Divine Providence is related and closely connected with the intellect, because Providence can only proceed from an intelligent being, from a being that is itself the most perfect Intellect. (ibid)

Maimonides then takes an additional step in his explanation that clearly distinguishes his position from that of Rabbi Dessler with regards to the impact of causation in human affairs. He states in the next chapter of the "Guide for the Perplexed":

> Hence it follows, in accordance with what I have mentioned in the preceding chapter, that the greater the share in which a person has obtained of this Divine influence, on account of both his physical predisposition and his training, the greater must also be the effect of Divine Providence upon him, for the action of Divine Providence is proportional to the endowment of intellect, as has been mentioned above. The relation of Divine Providence is therefore not the same to all men; the greater the human perfection a person has attained, the greater the benefit he derives from Divine Providence. This benefit is very great in the case of prophets, and varies according to the degree of their prophetic faculty; as it varies in the case of pious and good men according to their piety and uprightness. For it is the intensity of the Divine intellectual influence that has inspired the prophets, guided the good in their actions, and perfected the wisdom of the pious. In the same proportion as ignorant and disobedient person are deficient in that Divine influence, their condition is inferior, and their rank equal to that of irrational beings; and they are "like unto the beasts" (Psalm 44:21). (Book 3: Chapter 17)

Maimonides view is that natural law also applies and acts in the human being's life, to the extent that the person is not endowed with the intellectual influence. There are gradations of divine influence in a person's life depending on their level of development. Moses had the highest level of providential influence (direct intervention by God), as the greatest prophet and it decreases for other individuals from there. It would certainly seem to be the case that Maimonides holds that many individuals in the world are governed entirely by the laws of causation, as their low level of development equates them with beasts, as Maimonides states, for whom Divine Providence only relates to the species as a whole.

The Concept of "*Hester Panim*"

A concept relevant to our discussion which is also an established part of Jewish tradition is that of "*Hester Panim*" or "God's Hiding His Face". Rabbi Soloveitchik has commented extensively that the Holocaust would fall under this category. In this case, the sins of Jewish people result in God withdrawing His providential influence and allowing natural forces to operate. This is a form of punishment that can result in much more devastating outcomes than that of God's direct punishment. When God directly punishes, it is with a degree of mercy and the punishment is not sadistic or unbearable as its purpose is to bring the Jewish people to repentance. It is similar to the punishment of a concerned parent. But "*Hester Panim*" would be more parallel to a parent sending a child away from the home due to his or her sins. Once the person is "out in the world" unprotected, there is no limit to the suffering they may endure from the natural forces and evil of people inflicted upon them. He explains:

> There are two levels of Divine punishment, *Middat Hadin* and *Hester Panim*. The former involves measure for measure punishment, commensurate with one's sins. It does not signify God's withdrawal; on the contrary, it reflects His involvement and concern, intended to

stimulate *teshuvah* (repentance). *Middat Hadin*, therefore, never inflicts annihilation or total extermination, *kelayah*. *Hester Panim*, however, is a temporary suspension of God's active surveillance. He turns His back, so to speak, on events and leaves matters to chance. Under such circumstances, the usual vulnerability of the Jew invites the threat of total extermination. This is strikingly conveyed by the words *vehyahale-ekhol*, "they shall be devoured." What ensues is not circumscribed by consideration of measure for measure, and the magnitude and severity can be devastating. Without God's governing control, events may simply go beserk....The *Asarah Haruge Malkhut (*10 martyrs-RB*)* were victims of *Middat Hadin*, not *Hester Panim*. It was a measured *onesh* (punishment-RB), but it indicated God's involvement, *gezarah hi milefanai*. It is related in the *Eleh Ezharah* piyyut of the Yom Kippur Musaph service that, when the angels protested against the torturing to death of the Sages, a heavenly voice replied: 'If I hear further protest, I will force the world to revert to water. I will reduce the world to *tohu vavohu' (*RB-chaos and disorder*)* God threatened the *tohu vavohu* of *Hester Panim* if the *Middat Hadin* of controlled retribution were not accepted. The Holocaust was *Hester Panim*. We cannot explain the Holocaust but we can, at least, classify it theologically, characterize it, even if we have no answer to the question "why?" The unbounded horrors represented the *tohu vavohu* anarchy of the pre-*yitzirah* state. This is how the world appears when God's moderating surveillance is suspended. The State of Israel, however, reflects God's return to active providence, the termination of *Hester Panim*." ("Reflections on the Rav"-Abraham Besdin- pages 36-37)

The Rav is stating that when "Hester Panim" is in place, natural law controls the situation for a human being life and for that of the nation. This too seems to contradict my understanding of Rabbi Dessler's explanation of the Ramban and the Ibn Ezra's commentary on the Golden Calf.

The Implication of There Not Being True Causation

Without commenting on the validity of Rabbi Dessler's perspective that natural causation is an illusion, I do feel strongly that this perspective can be utilized by a person to justify behavior that is contrary to the Torah's objectives. Although one can argue that the seeing of everything being solely in the control of God's direct intervention will focus one's attention on keeping the *mitzvot*, it can also be used to minimize the responsibility one takes for the impact of personal destructive behavior. A person can reflect that he or she is never really the cause of anything, including the seemingly destructive and neglectful behaviors that they seem to perpetrate. For example, it may look like my negligent parenting was the cause of my child's destruction, but really it was not the cause. It was God's direct intervention. I did not cause my own failures in learning or my health-this was also directly decreed by God. I also cannot really help a person in need because my *chesed* or charity is not truly causative in their improvement. The person can say that the feeling of responsibility is an illusion and even a destructive delusion which I must try to see through to obtain a higher spiritual level. The doctor does not help heal the patient! The mother does not help soothe the feeling of the child! All is an illusionary situation constructed for the sake of my exercising of free will. I am supposed to act as if it is real, but at the same time know that it is isn't and that causation is an illusion. I must question whether this situation can really even function to allow me to exercise my free will if I know that my free will does not really impact the world around me at all and that to think that it does is a sign of my deficiency in understanding God's Providence!

A Different Explanation of the Sin of the Golden Calf

I would like to conclude this analysis with a different explanation for the nature of the sin perpetrated by the Golden Calf. Perhaps the destructive nature of the Golden Calf can be viewed as a profound distortion by the Jewish people of the concept of holiness. All of Judaism rests on the idea that there is true holiness in the world and that this holiness is related to the connection something has to the Creator. The greater the connection, it seems, the greater the holiness. The *Mishkan* became the holiest place on Earth and the Ark (*Aron HaKodesh*) the holiest place within the *Mishkan*. The *Kohanim* and the *Leviim* became the holiest people, assigned to attending the *Mishkan* and later the Temple. But perhaps this idea of levels of holiness was a post-Golden Calf phenomenon that became necessary due to the lowered level of the people caused by this incident. Perhaps in truth, all of existence has an equal holiness as it is all the creation of God and resulted from a single act of Creation. But the Jewish people, without Moses there, needed a focal point of their connection to God. This was the Golden Calf. They created a "holy object", inaccurately establishing the idea that one creation was more holy than another creation, when in truth all were creations of God and in one category.

The whole system of the *Mishkan* and all that was connected with it was, perhaps, a concession to this imprecise notion of holiness that became inculcated in the Jewish people due to the Golden Calf event. There had to be a hierarchy of holiness at this point, in order for the Jewish people to endure. This then became the root of the "debate" between God and Moses as to whether the Jewish people should continue to exist. The role of the Jewish people was to teach a correct concept of holiness to the world and now they were incapable of doing so. Therefore, why should they continue?

They will now perpetuate a falsehood! Somehow Moses "convinced" God that with proper reorientation and Moses' changed role, their purpose could be salvaged as teacher of the concept of holiness, though they would never achieve their original intent.

The Breaking of the *Luchos*

A question that comes to mind was the nature of the *luchos* (the Tablets with the 10 commandments/statements) and their being broken by Moshe upon descending the mountain. If I am posing the idea that the concept of differing degrees of holiness in the creation was a post-Golden Calf concession, but not the original intent of the Torah, then what was the purpose of the original *luchos* that Moshe brought down and then decided to destroy? I would like to suggest that the *luchos* were not brought down as an object of holiness for the people to reflect on. Instead, the role of the *luchos* was to establish with absolute certainty, the covenant between God and the Jewish people. Their miraculous nature showed the truth of that covenant without any question and may have changed the history of the Jewish people, by preventing the exile from occurring. But when Moshe saw the Golden Calf and understood it to be the Jewish people's desire for a hierarchy of holiness, he understood that the *luchos* would be taken as the holiest of objects and would be destructive to promoting the true concept of universal holiness throughout creation. He therefore decided to destroy them.

In conclusion, I would like to quote from the blessings before the morning *Shema* in which the angels express the true nature of holiness from their exalted perspective. It states:

> May your Name be praised forever, our King, Who forms ministering angels; Whose ministering angels all stand at the summit of the universe and proclaim-with awe,

together, loudly-the words of the living God and King of the universe. They are all beloved; they are all flawless; they are all mighty; they all do the will of their Maker with dread and reverence-They all open their mouth in holiness and purity, in song and hymn and bless praise, glorify, revere, sanctify, and declare the kingship of the Name of God, the mighty and awesome King; holy in He. Then they all accept upon themselves the yoke of heavenly sovereignty from one another, and grant permission to one another to sanctify the One Who formed them, with tranquility, with clear speech and with sweetness. All of them as one proclaim His holiness and say with awe:

Holy, holy holy is God, Master of Legions, the whole world is filled with His glory.

POETRY ON THE PARSHA

To See a World in a Grain of Sand (Fragments from "Songs of Innocence") by William Blake

To see a World in a Grain of Sand
And a Heaven in a Wild Flower,
Hold Infinity in the palm of your hand
And Eternity in an hour.

A Robin Redbreast in a Cage
Puts all Heaven in a Rage.
A dove house fill'd with doves and pigeons
Shudders Hell thro' all its regions.
A Dog starv'd at his Master's Gate
Predicts the ruin of the State.
A Horse misus'd upon the Road
Calls to Heaven for Human blood.
Each outcry of the hunted Hare
A fiber from the Brain does tear.

He who shall train the Horse to War
Shall never pass the Polar Bar.
The Beggar's Dog and Widow's Cat,

Feed them and thou wilt grow fat.
The Gnat that sings his Summer song
Poison gets from Slander's tongue.
The poison of the Snake and Newt
Is the sweat of Envy's Foot.

A truth that's told with bad intent
Beats all the Lies you can invent.
It is right it should be so;
Man was made for Joy and Woe;
And when this we rightly know
Thro' the World we safely go.

Every Night and every Morn
Some to Misery are Born.
Every Morn and every Night
Some are Born to sweet delight.
Some are Born to Endless Night.

God in All by Yehudah Halevi (excerpt)

Lord where shall I find Thee?
High and hidden is Thy place;
And where shall I not find Thee?
The world is full of Thy glory?
Found in the innermost being,
He set up the ends of the Earth:
The refuge for the year,
The trust for those far off.
Thou dwelleth among the Cherubim,
Thou abides in the clouds;
Thou art praised by Thine hosts
Yet art raised above their praise.
The whirling worlds cannot contain Thee;
How then the chambers of a Temple?

Hymn of the Fate of the Soul by Nachmanides (Ramban) (excerpt)

(The Soul):From the very beginning, before time long past,
I was stored among the hidden treasures.
He had brought me froth from nothing, but in the end of time,
 I shall be summoned back before the King.
My life flowed out of the depths of the spheres which gave me form and order.
Divine forces shaped me to be treasured in the chambers of the King.
Then He appeared to bring me out of hiding. He drove me out from all sides, made me descend the steps leading down from the pool of Shelah to the garden of the King.

PAINTINGS ON THE PARSHA

**Moses Receives the Law:
The Israelites Worship the Golden Calf**

Book of Vices and Virtues - 1279; British Library Add MS 54 180 Moses (with horns) receives the Law from God and he immediately sees the Children of Israel worshiping the Calf, and breaks the Tablets. Worship is kneeling before the image and blowing trumpets to honor and proclaim the golden deity. (R.M.)

Adoration of the Golden Calf – by Gerit de Wett (ca 1640)

Ecstatic worship is expressed in dancing around the image atop the column and making music. Drinking leads to debauchery in the foreground. (R.M.)

The Golden Calf - Poussin (1634) - National Gallery, London

The artist utilized the figures from his own painting of a pagan celebration (Bacchanalian Revel before Pan) to depict the Hebrew worship of the calf. (R.M.)

Angry Moses and the Golden Calf - by Richard McBee (1997)

Moses is furious at the Jewish people's sin of idolatry, smashing the sacred tablets that God gave them to the ground as the text's letters flew off and returned to their heavenly abode. (R.M.)

VAYAKHEL
CREATIVITY, SABBATH AND THE MISHKAN

The parsha begins in an unusual way with the statement by Moses that "These are the things that the Lord commanded to make" (35:1) followed by the verse: "Six days work may be done, but on the seventh you shall have sanctity, a day of complete rest to the Lord" (35:2). After this Moses warns the people not to kindle a fire on the Sabbath (35:3). Why is it only after this that the Torah returns to the items and materials for the making of the *Mishkan*?

Logically, it would seem that the statement "These are the things that the Lord commanded to make- לעשת א תָם (35:1) should come after the statements regarding the Sabbath and the prohibition of kindling fire on that day. These items (the sanctuary and fire) are not things to make - just the opposite: these are precise the things not to make on the Sabbath. The Torah states:

1. Moses called the whole community of the children of Israel to assemble, and he said to them: "These are the things that the Lord commanded to make.	וַיַּקְהֵל מֹשֶׁה אֶת כָּל עֲדַת בְּנֵי יִשְׂרָאֵל וַיֹּאמֶר אֲלֵהֶם אֵלֶּה הַדְּבָרִים
2. Six days work may be done, but on the seventh day you shall have sanctity, a day of complete rest to the Lord; whoever performs work thereon [on this day] shall be put to death.	שֵׁשֶׁת יָמִים תֵּעָשֶׂה מְלָאכָה וּבַיּוֹם הַשְּׁבִיעִי יִהְיֶה לָכֶם קֹדֶשׁ שַׁבַּת שַׁבָּתוֹן לַיהוָה כָּל הָעֹשֶׂה בוֹ מְלָאכָה יוּמָת:

3. You shall not kindle fire in any of your dwelling places on the Sabbath day."	לֹא תְבַעֲרוּ אֵשׁ בְּכֹל מֹשְׁבֹתֵיכֶם
10. And every wise hearted person among you shall come and make everything that the Lord has commanded:	וְכָל חֲכַם לֵב בָּכֶם יָבֹאוּ וְיַעֲשׂוּ אֵת כָּל
11. The Mishkan, its tent and its cover, its clasps and its planks, its bars, its pillars, and its sockets;	אֶת הַמִּשְׁכָּן אֶת אָהֳלוֹ וְאֶת מִכְסֵהוּ אֶת קְרָסָיו וְאֶת קְרָשָׁיו אֶת בְּרִיחָו אֶת עַמֻּדָיו

Isaac ben Judah Abravanel, the great Portuguese rationalist Torah scholar (1437–1508) states:

> If it is true that Moses assembled all Israel to command them regarding the work of the Tabernacle as the text has it "these are the words the Lord has commanded that you should do them"–why did he begin with the commandment of the Sabbath: "six days shall work be done but on the seventh day they shall be to you a holy day"? This commandment had already been imparted on the descent of the manna and in the Decalogue on Mount Sinai and in the course of instructions concerning the Tabernacle. Why did it have to be repeated here again?

Abravanel, commenting on the previous parsha, *Ki Tissa* provides an answer to his question:

> Since the Tabernacle and its appurtenances whose making God had commanded symbolized communion with Him and the resting of his Presence on the nation, we might have thought that this activity out-weighed in importance all the other Biblical prescriptions, and most certainly the Sabbath rest. For perfection lies in action and performance is more perfect than non-performance and rest. This is especially true when such a sacred and sublime performance as that of building a Tabernacle is involved….In addition, actual work is a more eloquent witness of faith than cessation from work, since action is positive and inaction negation….On this account, the Lord told Moses to say to Israel: verily you shall keep My Sabbaths, i.e. though the work of the Tabernacle is sacred and of great importance in My eyes, nevertheless you must not override the Sabbath, on its account, but observe it.

The Abravanel explains why the statement regarding the Sabbath is necessary, but does not explain why the seeming lesser act of Sabbath restraint "trumps" the building of the Tabernacle. I would like to explore the idea which the Abravanel focuses on: the contrast and comparison of action and restraint from action.

Active &Passive Aspects of Our Relationship with God

To delve deeper into the idea of activity and passivity in the religious experience, we can gain much by briefly recounting main points of Rabbi Joseph B. Solovetichik's well-known essay "The Lonely Man of Faith" where he describes the human being as having two essentially conflicting dimensions to his or her personality. He terms these two fundamental aspects of the human soul, "Adam the first" and "Adam the second". These names correspond with the Adam depicted in the first chapter of Genesis (*Bereisheit*) –"Adam the first", and the Adam we meet in the second chapter of Bereisheit- "Adam the second". We will see that "Adam the first" is essentially active and "Adam the second" is essentially passive in his relationship with God.

The Adam the first dimension of the human personality is the part of the person's inner self that seeks to conquer and reshape the world to address his physical, social and psychological needs. This is in accordance with bringing to fruition God's command to human being that they should "be fruitful and multiply and conquer the Earth", placing it under their dominion. The Rav describes this as Adam the first's legitimate quest for a "dignified existence". He states:

> Man is an honorable being. In other words, man is a dignified being and to be human means to live with dignity. However, this equation of two unknown qualities, requires further elaboration. We must be ready to answer the question: what is dignity and how can it be realized? The answer we find again in the words of the Psalmist, who addressed himself to this obvious question and who termed man not only as honorable but also a glorious being, spelling out the essence of glory in unmistakable terms: "Thou hast made him to have dominion over the works of Thy hands. Thou hast put all things under his feet." In other words, dignity was equated by the Psalmist with man's capability of dominating his environment and exercising control over it. Man acquires dignity through glory, through his *majestic* posture vis-à-vis his environment (Lonely Man of Faith pp. 14-15).

The Rav makes clear that this pursuit of dignity which drives man to act and impact the world around him, and transform it to a domain that addresses his needs, is a sanctioned path of action. He states:

> In doing all this, Adam the first is trying to carry out the mandate entrusted to him by his Maker who, at dawn of the sixth mysterious day of creation, addressed Himself to man and summoned him to "fill the earth and subdue it." It is God who decreed that the story of Adam the first be the great saga of freedom of man-slave who gradually transforms himself into man- master (Lonely Man of Faith p. 19).

The Rav, while making clear that the Torah sanctions this creative "drive" in the human soul, also notes its limitations with regards to man's relationship with God. He states:

> He is this worldly-minded, finitude-oriented, beauty-centered. Adam the first is always an aesthete, whether engaged in an intellectual or an ethical performance. His conscience is energized not by the idea of the good, but by that of the beautiful. His mind is questing not for the true, but for the pleasant and functional, which are rooted in the aesthetical, not the noetic-ethical sphere. (Lonely Man of Faith, p. 19)

The passion of Adam the first is not for a communion with God, but for the carrying out of his projects. Building human civilization, beautifying it, understanding it - all these things fascinate him. Even his quest to understand the secrets of creation, the wisdom of the Torah and what are God's ways of interacting with His creation, all take on the character of a desire for mastery. The Rav states:

> While pursuing this goal, driven by an urge which he cannot but obey, Adam the first transcends the limits of the reasonable and probable and ventures into the open spaces of a boundless universe. Even this longing for vastness, no matter how adventurous and fantastic, is legitimate. Man, reaching for the distant stars is acting in harmony with his

nature which was created, willed, and directed by his Maker. It is a manifestation of obedience to rather than rebellion against God. (Lonely Man of Faith p. 20)

The Rav contrasts this Adam the first persona with that of Adam the second:

> However, while the cosmos provokes Adam the first to quest for power and control, thus making him ask the functional "how" question, Adam the second responds to the call of the cosmos by engaging in a different kind of cognitive gesture. He doesn't ask a single functional question. (Lonely Man of Faith, p. 21)

> This Adam the second experience is a particular type of willed passivity-an allowance of oneself to be conquered and "defeated" by God. It has its source in a deep inner realization that one's being is nothing without God and nothing in comparison with God. This experience of Adam the second is antithetical to the quest for dignity that we cited as the core mission of Adam the first. Cathartic redemptiveness, in contrast to dignity, cannot be attained through man's acquisition of control of his environment, but through man's exercise of control over himself. A redeemed life is ipso facto a disciplined life. While a dignified life is attained by majestic man who courageously surges forward and confronts mute nature- a lower form of being-in a mood of defiance, redemption is achieved when humble man makes a movement of recoil, and lets himself be confronted and defeated by a Higher and Truer Being." (Lonely Man of Faith, p. 36)

The Rav makes clear that the Adam the first's active experience is one that appreciates God and obeys God, but is not the source of one's "living" experience of God. The personal connection that an individual has with God, according to Rabbi Soloveitchik, is part of man's essential inner being and is experienced only when one surrenders one's self to God and places one's whole self at the disposal of the Creator. The Rav states:

> The Biblical metaphor referring to God breathing life into Adam alludes to the actual preoccupation of the latter with God, to his genuine living experience of God rather than to some divine potential or endowment in Adam symbolized by *imago Dei*. (Lonely Man of Faith, pp. 23-24)

In light of the Rav's insight we can now revisit the problem of the verse that seems to unnecessarily insert the prohibition of violating the Sabbath immediately before the description of building the sanctuary. The Abravanel we quoted earlier, explained that the verse was needed to counter the assumption we might have that the construction of the sanctuary, as a positive act of service to God would outweigh and neutralize the need to passively confirm our belief in God as Creator, which we accomplish with the Sabbath. As we quoted the Abravanel earlier:

> Since the Tabernacle and its appurtenances symbolized communion with Him and the resting of his Presence on the nation, we might have thought that this activity out-weighed in importance all the other Biblical prescriptions, and most certainly the Sabbath rest. For perfection lies in action, and performance is greater perfection than non-performance and rest.

The perspective of the "Lonely Man of Faith" analysis does not place activity over passivity in the service of God. Even though the Rav does not state whether Adam the first or Adam the second is superior to the other, in my opinion, the greater of the two dimensions of the human soul rests with Adam the second. The Rav is making clear that Judaism certainly does not hold that man is supposed to refrain from actively reshaping the world to make it a more just and pleasant place to live. This is our right and our duty as human beings. But what the Rav calls man's "genuine living experience of God" and his personal redemption, comes with his decision to allow God to defeat him and to accept the "yoke of Heaven" and the absolute servitude to the One True Being. Passivity, at least this particular heroic passivity, is the greater spiritual "act" so to speak, as it transforms a person to one who "dwells with God" and who realizes that a person's fulfillment is not due to his accomplishments, but from the gift of his relationship with God. In the "Lonely Man of Faith" essay, the Rav describes the covenantal community of the Jewish people as a nation that not only serves God but participates in a community of which God is a member.

So perhaps we can see that the building of the Sanctuary, reflective of the human need to serve God through creative action, is logically outweighed by the Sabbath, a day when man's decides to refrain from creativity and to focus on his role as a servant of the One True Creator and bask in the joy of our ability to have a relationship with the only Real Existent which we call God.

Fire and Creativity

The second issue we raised at the beginning of this analysis was the reason why the prohibition against making fire was stated at the beginning of this *parsha*, prior to the description of the construction of the sanctuary. To review the first three verses of the *parsha* are:

1. Moses called the whole community of the children of Israel to assemble, and he said to them: "These are the things that the Lord commanded to make.	א. וַיַּקְהֵל מֹשֶׁה אֶת כָּל עֲדַת בְּנֵי יִשְׂרָאֵל וַיֹּאמֶר אֲלֵהֶם אֵלֶּה הַדְּבָרִים אֲשֶׁר צִוָּה יְהֹוָה לַעֲשֹׂת אֹתָם:

2. Six days work may be done, but on the seventh day you shall have sanctity, a day of complete rest to the Lord; whoever performs work thereon [on this day] shall be put to death.	ב שֵׁ֣שֶׁת יָמִים֮ תֵּעָשֶׂ֣ה מְלָאכָה֒ וּבַיּ֣וֹם הַשְּׁבִיעִ֗י יִהְיֶ֨ה לָכֶ֥ם קֹ֛דֶשׁ שַׁבַּ֥ת שַׁבָּת֖וֹן לַיהוָ֑ה כָּל־הָעֹשֶׂ֥ה ב֛וֹ מְלָאכָ֖ה יוּמָֽת׃
3. You shall not kindle fire in any of your dwelling places on the	ג לֹא־תְבַעֲר֣וּ אֵ֔שׁ בְּכֹ֖ל מֹשְׁבֹתֵיכֶ֑ם

These three verses are followed by the statement by Moses regarding the people's donation of goods and services to the construction of the sanctuary.

The great Italian commentator Ovadiah ben Jacob Sforno (1475–1550) focuses on the issue that fire is a destructive force and one might think that making it is not prohibited by the Sabbath prohibition against the 39 types of creative work done in the construction of the sanctuary. Sforno comments on this verse Shemot 35:3:

> Even though kindling fire is on the whole destructive, nevertheless, since it makes all, or most, forms of work possible, it is forbidden on the Shabbat.

Reflecting on Sforno's idea, fire takes a central role in the creativity of human civilization. It is the source and force of the creative acts that makes possible Adam the first's "dignified life" we discussed earlier in our review of Rabbi Soloveitchik's essay "Lonely Man of Faith". Most of us are familiar with the Greek myth of Prometheus who, as the tale goes, stole fire from Zeus and brought it to man. In the Western classical tradition, Prometheus became a figure who represented human striving, particularly the quest for scientific knowledge. From the perspective that the making of fire represents the striving and conquests of man over the environment and his creative endeavor to build human civilization, its being singled out with regards to the Sabbath can be seen as defining the Sabbath as the time that man, as we said earlier, refrains from this striving and recognizes that God is the One True Creator who brought the world to being from nothingness. Man is permitted a certain hubris and self-aggrandizement during the six days of the week when he is fulfilling his God-given mission of "be fruitful and multiply and conquer the Earth." But on the Sabbath, the fire is extinguished, and man's role as "transformer" and "re-shaper" of the world is put aside. He takes his place as a humble servant of God, focusing his attention and awe upon the greatness of the Creator.

POETRY ON THE PARSHA

Light a Candle by Zelda (translated from the Hebrew)

Light a candle. Drink wine.
Softly the Sabbath has plucked the sinking sun.
Slowly the Sabbath descends, the rose of heaven in her hand.
How can the Sabbath plant a huge and shining flower in a blind and narrow heart? How can the Sabbath plant a bud of angels in a heart of raving flesh?
Can the rose of eternity grow in a generation enslaved to destruction, A generation enslaved to death?

Yearning for God (A Song of the Sons of Korach) Psalm 42

As the deer longs for running waters, so does my soul long for You, O God! My soul thirsts for God, for the living God; when shall I come before God?
My tears have been my food day and night, as people taunt me, day after day: "Where is your God?"
I pour out my soul when I recall how I marched in the procession, Moving slowly towards the house of God, with joyous shouts of praise, Amidst the festive throng.
Why are you so desolate my soul, why so distraught within me? Hope in God. For I shall still praise Him for His saving presence.

The Lord in My Portion by Judah Halevi

The slaves of time are the slaves of a slave; Only the slave of the Lord is free.
Therefore, while other men seek their portion, 'The Lord is my portion' says my soul.

Sabbath Song by Anonymous

Old and grey as I am, I hurry forth on Friday, filled with love to meet the Sabbath. My joy approaches, my grief disappears and I sing out: 'Welcome!'
For love of this day, I purify my soul, I bless the Lord. I leap and dance,
'Yes this is it!' A foretaste of the world to come!' Make the words of the seers come true, my God. Hasten the advent of the King, Priest and Prophet majestic in splendor.

PAINTING ON THE PARSHA

Blessing the Shabbos Candles – by Isidore Kaufmann

Kaufmann (1853 – 1921) was a Viennese artist who specialized in depictions of Eastern European traditional Jewish society, concentrating on the psychological inner life of his subjects. On this summer Friday night the room is filled with light and purity of the approaching Shabbos as the wife awaits her husband's return from synagogue to join her in the events of the holy day., the foremost of which is actively refraining from any prohibited labor.

And the Holy One, blessed is He, Came
by Archie Rand (2006)

Archie Rand created a series of 10 paintings representing each of the 10 refrains of the Passover song Had Gadya. The last line of this ultimately horrifying ditty that escalates increasingly violent forms of destruction presents God Himself defeating Death. It is the moment of final peace and union with the Divine. In Rand's painting it is the moment Shabbos arrives.

PEKUDEI
CREATIVITY & THE POWER OF GOLD

The parsha of Pekudei states the amount of gold required for the sanctuary:

24. All the gold that had been used for the work in all the work of the Holy the gold of the waving was twenty nine talents, seven hundred and thirty shekels, according to the holy shekel.	כד. כָּל הַזָּהָב הֶעָשׂוּי לַמְּלָאכָה בְּכֹל מְלֶאכֶת הַקֹּדֶשׁ וַיְהִי ׀ זְהַב הַתְּנוּפָה תֵּשַׁע וְעֶשְׂרִים כִּכָּר וּשְׁבַע מֵאוֹת וּשְׁלֹשִׁים שֶׁקֶל בְּשֶׁקֶל הַקֹּדֶשׁ:

The other two metals utilized from the sanctuary are silver (*kesef*) and copper (*nechoshet*).

The majority of the gold was utilized for the following items of the sanctuary:
1-The holy ark – wood coated inside and outside with gold.
2- the ark cover- pure gold.
3-The spice altar –wood coated on outside with gold.
4-The menorah- beaten from a single piece of gold.
5-The table for the showbread-wood coated on outside with gold.
6-Parts of the *Kohane Gadole's* clothing.
7-Additional small utensils of the sanctuary.

It is quite clear that gold is the metal used for those objects designated as most holy. The center of the sanctuary and the area most restricted for use or entry in the "Holy of Holies" which contain the holy ark and the ark cover, both of which are made of gold. The "Holy" which was the area immediately outside of the "Holy of Holies" contained the golden spice altar and the menorah, both of which were gold.

No silver or copper were used here. Outside of the Holy is the sanctuary courtyard was the washing basin and the altar on which the sacrifices were offered. These were both made of copper (some translate as bronze, which is a copper/tin alloy). Silver was primarily utilized for the bases of the pillars that made up the structure of the sanctuary. But it is gold that is used for objects endowed with the highest level of holiness.

Why is gold the metal of choice for this purpose? Although very beautiful and enduring, gold has many negative connotations, the most prominent one being its use for the golden calf which the Jewish people constructed when they surmised that Moses delayed in descending from Mount Sinai. This sin is often regarded as the most damaging one in our history. Also, gold was associated with the Pharaoh's and Egypt, from whose idolatrous and lascivious culture the Jews were rescued in their redemption from Egypt. One could certainly ask whether there are any positive associations with gold that make it the material of choice from turning ones thoughts to God? There is a very intriguing statement in the *Shemos Raba* 51:6 which states:

> Aaron said to them: "Break off the gold rings…" (Shemot 32:2). And the people broke off their golden rings and showered them upon him until he was compelled to exclaim: "Enough!" This was the point of Moses' rebuke "And Laban, and Hazerot, and Dizahab" (Devarim 1:2)- (*Dizahab is a hint as it can be read to mean "enough gold"*) This can be compared to a young man who came to a city and found the people collecting money for charity, and when they asked him also to subscribe, he went on giving until they had to tell him that he had already given enough. Further on his travels, he came to a place where they were collecting for a theater, and when asked to contribute toward it, he was also so generous that he had to be told, "Enough!". Israel, likewise, contributed so much toward the Golden Calf that they had to be told, "Enough!" And they contributed so much gold to Mishkan that they had to be told,

"Enough!" as it is said, "For their efforts had been more than enough for all the tasks to be done." (37:7). The Holy One Blessed be He then said: "Let the gold of the Mishkan atone for the gold they brought toward making of the Golden Calf".

Avivah Zornberg in her book "The Particulars of Rapture-Reflections of Exodus" notes a subtle point in that the midrash's parallel example for the gold of the calf and the *mishkan* until they are told "enough!" is that of a man who gives gold to charity and then, afterwards gives gold to the theater, until he is told in both cases, "enough!" Ms. Zornberg explains that in the case of the man with the gold given to the charity and the theater the order is reversed from that of the Golden Calf and the Mishkan to dispel the idea that there was some positive development in the case of the Jews "over-giving" for the *mishkan* after the previous "over-giving" to the calf. In the case of the man in the midrash, he gives first to charity and afterwards to the theater, reversing the order of the Jewish people making clear that no repentance or development took place between the two donations in the case of the Jewish people either. Ms. Zornberg states:

> In effect, however, the inverted parable sets up a tension between narrative and parable, between mashal and nimshal. The sequence is confused, so that a simple optimism about right objects replacing wrong objects becomes impossible. The story of the young man, with his compulsive, morally opaque generosity, seeps into the midrashic narrative of the people. A linear progression from evil to good forms of energy is undermined in the parable structure, where the time sequence cannot objectively indicate redemption or atonement. It is only God's words that retroactively restructure the events of the past expressing a "wish" that *this* should cover *that*. God's words are in the jussive form: "Let it be…" Without His words, the facts carry no unequivocal meaning.

> Essentially, God suggests a possible world, imposing order on the promiscuous generosity of His undiscriminating people. (p. 468).

I would like to suggest another idea indicated by the *midrash*. Why did the gold of the *mishkan* atone for the gold of the calf? Perhaps this *midrash* helps to clarify that the degradation of the Jewish people's perspective which occurred with the golden calf to require the worship of God in a manner that partook of place and the creation of their own hands, needed to be rectified in some manner. This need could not be reversed to the pre-calf level. But now the question was how to carry out this worship in a manner that was not so far from the truth that it remained idolatrous. The inclusion of place and man-made objects had to be optimally included in the act of worshipping God. Once the people were at a level that required place and objects of their own making to draw their attention to God, what was the best manner in which such a place and such objects could be made? This manner was the place and the structure and materials of the *mishkan*. This was why it was , *so* to speak, an "atonement" or, more precisely, an optimal sublimation of the desire for physicality in worship.

The worship was now directed to a place-this place being the *mishkan* which was associated with the propitious acts which took place there, such as the offering of Isaac by Abraham in absolute servitude to God. This *miskan* had the holy ark at its core. Within the ark was the "*aseret hadibros*" (the tablets of the 10 commandments or, more accurately, the 10 statements.) So at the heart of the *mishkan* was not an image, but a set on laws based on concepts which were abstract in nature and not at all physical. In this way the gold of the *mishkan* redeemed the gold of the calf. The gold that remained physical in the golden calf, here housed the "*aseret hadibros*" ("ten commandments") and the physical gold was made to serve that which was of true value-the connection to non-physical God through wisdom.

Many great commentators have explained the use of gold in the *mishkan* based on its unique qualities. For example, gold represents purity and eternity in that it does not tarnish or change by mixing with other elements like silver and copper do. However, I would suggest that the gold is also simply alluring and attractive because of its beauty, rarity and historical association with wealth and grandeur. It was the metal of the powerful, the wealthy, the royal. As such, it was the best material to attract one's attention to that which was truly most precious. Now the physical gold of the *miskhan* attracted the human mind to the true value - the worship of God and the inculcation of the ideas of the Torah represented by the tablets within the holy ark.

The redeeming of the gold of the calf takes place because gold which previously drew man's mind away from the truth (in the case of the Golden Calf) was now utilized to bring man back to focusing on that which is of true value-the worship of the One True Being who is the source of all value through the ideas within the Torah (represented by the *aseres hadibros*).

Regarding the solid gold ark cover with the two cherub figures, the Torah states:

> Betzalel made the ark of shittim wood, two and a half cubits long, a cubit and a half wide, and a cubit and a half high. He overlaid it with pure gold within and without, and made a rim of gold to it round about ... He made the covering of pure gold, two and a half cubits long and a cubit and a half wide. He made two keruvim of gold, hammered out of one piece, at the two ends of the covering: one keruv at one end and the other keruv at the

other end; he made the keruvim of one piece with the covering, at its two ends. The keruvim had their wings spread out above, shielding the covering with their wings. They faced each other; the faces of the keruvim were turned toward the covering." (Exodus 37:1,2,6-9)

The two cherubs (*keruvim*) that are atop the ark cover and resemble two winged children facing each other and looking downward. Regarding these, the Shadal (Rabbi Shmuel David Luzzatto, Italy, 1800-1865) states:

> Prior to stating that [God] will meet with you and impart to you from above the covering ... the Torah states what is to be placed inside the ark, to teach us that the holiness of the ark stems from the stone tablets within it and not from its covering or from the keruvim.

Luzzato makes clear his opinion that the holiness of the ark came from what was within it- the *aseres hadibros* representing the Torah and its wisdom.

Creating a Place for God to Dwell

The *mishkan* was not a natural creation. It was the creation of human hands. This aspect of focusing on God through an object of human handicraft- even one whose form and materials were instructed by God, represented a lowering of the level of the Jewish people. Does God need to have a place or a particular, man-made structure through which He communicates his presence to the Jewish people? This was not needed on Mount Sinai, where all reached their highest level of contact with the Creator. But after the golden calf, another concession was needed to accommodate the lowering of the Jewish level of perception of God. Not only was a particular, designated place and objects required, but, in addition, the place and object needed to be assembled by human artifice. When God says to the Jewish people: "And they shall make a Sanctuary and I will dwell among them",

(Shemot 25:8) it is not inconsequential that the place that God will "dwell" is made by the Jewish people themselves. Why is this?

Man, as Rabbi Soloveitchik ("the Rav") clarifies so beautifully in his essay "Lonely Man of Faith", has two core dimensions to his personality. One is the builder and conqueror who takes his sanctioned place as the ruler and controller of his physical environment, utilizing his energies, intellect and drives to create a sophisticated human civilization. This dimension of the human personality, which Rabbi Soloveitchik termed "Adam the first" after the description of Adam in the first chapter of Bereisheit is how many uses his powers to transform the world into one that is not only pleasant and safe, but also just and merciful. It is permitted and required by the Creator. The Rav states:

> In doing all this, Adam the first is trying to carry out the mandate entrusted to him by his Maker who, at dawn of the sixth mysterious day of creation, addressed Himself to man and summoned him to "fill the earth and subdue it." It is God who decreed that the story of Adam the first be the great saga of freedom of man-slave who gradually transforms himself into man-master (Lonely Man of Faith p. 19).

Although Adam the first's activities are sanctioned and required, there are not how man truly clings to God. It is only through the allowance of God to completely conquer man, with man taking his place as God's willing and joyous servant in fulfillment of the covenant that man can enter into a relationship with the Creator. The Rav states:

> Cathartic redemptiveness, in contrast to dignity, cannot be attained through man's acquisition of control of his environment, but through man's exercise of control over himself. A redeemed life is ipso facto a disciplined life. While a dignified life is attained by majestic man who courageously

surges forward and confronts mute nature- a lower form of being-in a mood of defiance, redemption is achieved when humble man makes a movement of recoil, and lets himself be confronted and defeated by a Higher and Truer Being." (Lonely Man of Faith, p. 36)

When the Jewish people created the *mishkan* and incorporated a work of their own hands into their closest relationship with God (prayer, supplication and praise) they moved from an Adam the second experience of pure servitude, to one in which their craft and ingenuity entered the relationship. Man's power and capacity as a creator himself was injected into the relationship. This, in my opinion, was a lowering of the nature of the relationship as it now had aspects of man's attempt to "control God", so to speak. Similar to the motivation behind idolatry, by which he longs to "control the gods" through his a formulaic series of acts of worship, so too the service of God in the *mishkan* now contained the creations of man's hand and handiwork and gave man a greater sense of control and mastery over his own fate. This sense of control was a major dimension of the need to create the golden calf and its residue remained in the form of the *mishkan*, created by Betzalel and the Jewish people. As Yeshiyahu (Isaiah) stated in the name of God:

> So says the Lord, "The heavens are My throne, and the earth is My footstool; which is the house that you will build for Me, and which is the place of My rest? (66:1)

POETRY ON THE PARSHA

The Living Temple by Oliver Wendell Holmes Sr.

Not in the world of light alone, Where God has built his blazing throne,
Nor yet alone in earth below, with belted seas that come and go,
And endless isles of sunlit green, is all thy Maker's glory seen:
Look in upon thy wondrous frame,—Eternal wisdom still the same!
The smooth, soft air with pulse-like waves flows murmuring through its hidden caves,
Whose streams of brightening purple rush, fired with a new and livelier blush,
While all their burden of decay the ebbing current steals away,
And red with Nature's flame they start from the warm fountains of the heart.
No rest that throbbing slave may ask, forever quivering o'er his task,
While far and wide a crimson jet leaps forth to fill the woven net
Which in unnumbered crossing tides the flood of burning life divides,
Then, kindling each decaying part, Creeps back to find the throbbing heart.
But warmed with that unchanging flame behold the outward moving frame,
Its living marbles jointed strong with glistening band and silvery thong,
And linked to reason's guiding reins by myriad rings in trembling chains,
Each graven with the threaded zone which claims it as the master's own.
See how yon beam of seeming white is braided out of seven-hued light,
Yet in those lucid globes no ray by any chance shall break astray.
Hark how the rolling surge of sound, arches and spirals circling round,

Wakes the hushed spirit through thine ear with music it is heaven to hear.
Then mark the cloven sphere that holds all thought in its mysterious folds;
That feels sensation's faintest thrill, and flashes forth the sovereign will;
Think on the stormy world that dwells locked in its dim and clustering cells!
The lightning gleams of power it sheds along its hollow glassy threads!
O Father! grant thy love divine to make these mystic temples thine!
When wasting age and wearying strife have sapped the leaning walls of life,
When darkness gathers over all, and the last tottering pillars fall,
Take the poor dust thy mercy warms, and mould it into heavenly forms!

Where Shall I Find You? by Judah Halevi

Lord, where shall I find You? Your place is lofty and secret. And where shall I not find you?
The whole earth is full of Your glory!
You are found in man's innermost heart, yet You fixed earth's boundaries.
You are a strong tower for those who are near, and the trust of those who are far.
You are enthroned on the cherubim, yet You dwell in the heights of heaven.
You are praised by Your hosts, but even their praise is not worthy of You.
The sphere of heaven cannot contain You; how much less the chambers of the Temple!
Even when You rise above Your hosts on the throne, high and exalted,
You are nearer to them than their own bodies and souls.
Their mouths attest that they have no Maker except You.
Who shall not fear You? All bear the yoke of your kingdom.

And who shall not call to You? It is You who give them their food.

I have sought to come near You, I have called to You with all my heart;

And when I went out towards You, I found You coming towards me.

I look upon Your wondrous power with awe. Who can say that he has not seen You?

The heavens and their legions proclaim Your dread-without a sound.

But can God really dwell among men?

Their foundations are dust-what can they conceive of Him?

Yet You, O Holy One, make Your home where they sing Your praises and Your glory.

The living creatures, standing on the summit of the world, praise Your wonders.

Your throne is above their heads, yet it is You who carry them all!

PAINTINGS ON THE PARSHA

The Ark in Exile – by Shoshanna Golin

The Ark of the Covenant had a covering of pure gold crowned with a sculpture of two child-like winged figures. They faced one another and it was between them that God would rest His presence to be with the Jewish people. However, when the Children of Israel did not obey God, the kruvim faced away from each other, expressing the discord between God and His people. This was the matrix of the connection between the Divine and the Jewish people.

The Golden Calf – by Richard McBee (2010)

Jewish worshipers gather around the golden Christian image of the Lamb of God in misplaced devotion. Golden images are inherently dangerous and yet God commands us to place one in the Holy of Holies to teach us the terrifying proximity of the commanded to the forbidden.

INDEX OF IMAGES

All artwork by Richard McBee, oil on canvas except where noted

richardmcbee.com

Moses Kills the Egyptian (2010) 30 x 30 pg.

God Attacks Moses (2010) 30 x 30 pg.

Nahshon ben Amminadav Enters the Sea (2006) 20 x 20 pg.

Exodus (1999) 48 x 60 pg.

Covenant Between the Parts (2002) 20 x 20 pg.

Miriam saves the Infant Moses (2010) 30 x 30 pg.

The Plague of the First Born (2002) 20 x 20 pg.

Moses and Aaron Leading the People (1997) 12 x 40 pg.

Moses and Miriam Sing the Song at the Sea (2017) each 24 x 24 pg.

Sinai Mountain (1994) 68 x 68 pg.

Sinai Chuppah Fence (1998) 20 x 16 pg.

Elisha and the Shunemite Woman (1991) 40 x 30 pg.

Naomi and Ruth (1998) 24 x 30 pg.

Terumah by Archie Rand (1989) pg.

13th Century Perpignan Manuscript pg.

13th Century British Museum Miscellany pg.

Arch of Titus, Rome (82 CE) pg.

Aaron and the Temple, Dura Europos (235 CE) pg.

The High Priest and the Purification of the Leper by Botticelli (1483) pg.

Priests and the Lame Man by Domenico Tiepolo (ca. 1790) pg.

Haggadah (title page) by Aaron Wolf Herlingen of Gewitsch (1725) pg.

Aaron: Cohen Gadol – Monumental Sculpture (19th Century) **Artist Unknown** pg.

Moses Receives the Law: the Israelites Worship the Golden Calf (Book of Vices and Virtues (1279) British Library Add MS 54180 pg.

Adoration of the Golden Calf by Gerit de Wett (ca 1640) pg.

The Golden Calf by Poussin (1634) pg.

Angry Moses and the Golden Calf (R. McBee 1997) 68 x 84 pg.

Blessing the Shabbos Candles by Isidore Kaufman (ca 1890) pg.

And the Holy One, Blessed is He, Came by Archie Rand (2006) pg.

The Ark in Exile by Shoshanna Golin (1998) pg.

The Golden Calf (2010) 30 x 24 pg.

Cover Image

Exodus (1999) 48 x 60

www.ingramcontent.com/pod-product-compliance
Lightning Source LLC
Chambersburg PA
CBHW061645040426
42446CB00010B/1593